The Butterfly Chronicles

A Journey of Finding God's
Purpose Living with
A Rare Genetic Disorder

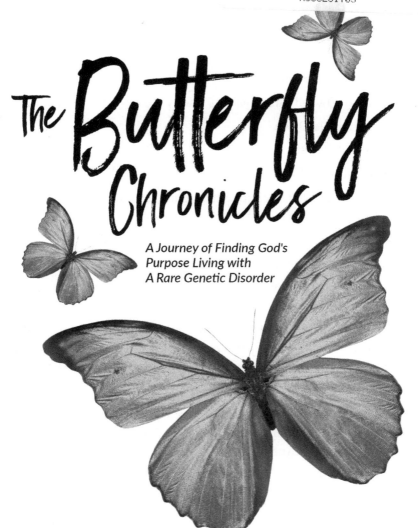

Nicole Irene Cleveland

Trilogy Christian Publishers

A Wholly Owned Subsidary of Trinity Broadcasting Network

2442 Michelle Drive

Tustin, CA 92780

For information, address Trilogy Christian Publishing

Rights Department, 2442 Michelle Drive, Tustin, Ca 92780.

Trilogy Christian Publishing/ TBN and colophon are trademarks of Trinity Broadcasting Network.

For information about special discounts for bulk purchases, please contact Trilogy Christian Publishing.

Manufactured in the United States of America

Trilogy Disclaimer: The views and content expressed in this book are those of the author and may not necessarily reflect the views and doctrine of Trilogy Christian Publishing or the Trinity Broadcasting Network.

10 9 8 7 6 5 4 3 2 1

Library of Congress Cataloging-in-Publication Data is available.

ISBN 978-1-68556-448-3

ISBN 978-1-68556-449-0 (ebook)

Dedication

I dedicate this book to my family, who from day one has been on this journey with me and has made numerous sacrifices so I could live the most normal and fulfilling life. I love each one of you, and this story is as much yours as it is mine.

To my fellow Turner syndrome butterflies, this is for you as well. I hope you will read this book and feel empowered to go out and achieve your goals. I also hope that you will see yourself in this story and feel understood.

CHAPTER 1

Navigating The Unknown

"Mr. and Mrs. Cleveland, we are going to have to perform an emergency delivery. Your baby's heart rate is dangerously high, and the baby is in fetal distress."

With those words, my mom was rushed into surgery for an emergency C-section. I was delivered shortly after on March 14, 1985. I was rushed to the NICU at St Luke's Hospital in Sioux City, Iowa. Neither my mom nor dad got to hold me. All they could keep asking after being told they had a daughter was "Is she going to be ok?" What should have been one of the happiest days of my parents' lives was suddenly turned in to a parent's worst nightmare. All my parents could do was lean on their faith and pray with their family and friends for support.

After a few days in the NICU. I suffered from jaundice, racing heart rate, and my hands and feet were swollen; the doctors knew something profoundly serious was causing these issues and my parents were in search for answers. The test results that they were given raised more questions than answers. After getting no answers, a doctor from the Children's Medical Center in Omaha, Nebraska was called in to perform a test called the karyotype. It is a test that does a snapshot of your genes, and it checks for abnormalities.

Along with this test, several others were performed. A few days later, my parents were informed that the karyotype results showed abnormalities.

I was diagnosed with the rare genetic disorder known as Turner syndrome. This is a rare genetic disorder that 1 in 2000 females have. It is in fact so rare that only one percent of women who are pregnant with a child with Turner syndrome will ever make it to full term. It could affect several major organs such as the heart and kidneys. It may also cause delayed motor skills development, hearing loss, vision loss, and learning disabilities. In almost all cases it causes infertility and below average height.

All this and more were laid out by specialist before my parents could even absorb the news that they would have to raise a child with special needs, and they were not even sure of what those needs would even be. What would their daughter's future even look like? Just days before, my parents were preparing and just hoping for a happy and healthy baby, overjoyed to be adding to their growing family. Now, they were dealt a hand they were not sure how to play. All they could do was lean on God for strength and guidance; they would often lean on the words of Isaiah 41:10, "So do not fear, for I am with you, do not be dismayed, for I am your God. I will strengthen you and help you; I will uphold you with my righteous right hand."

Thinking the worst and hoping for the best, my parents sought out the best medical experts and care Iowa had to offer, and a few months later my parents began to get a clearer picture of how this disorder of would affect me and what challenges would lie ahead. Not to say they were given all the answers but at least there was more insight and at least that was a starting point.

They were told I had mosaic Turner syndrome, a mild form of Turner syndrome and that I would begin to show the symptoms of it as I developed and grew. They were told it was a chromosome disorder that some of my X chromosomes were missing or deformed. The average girl should have forty-six xx chromosomes; I had forty-five normal chromosomes. My parents were told I may have to wear braces on my legs as I might not be able to walk normally. On top of this, speaking could be difficult for me. They were told to visit a genetic counselor who specialized in rare genetic disorders such as mine.

A genetic counselor is someone who helps families adjust to the challenges of being diagnosed with birth defects, disorders and other inherited conditions.

The months following my birth my parents began to find a routine, well as much of a routine one could have with a four-year-old son and an infant daughter. My mom stayed home and took care of my brother and I until I started school. She would have a small in-home daycare and would take care of the children in the neighborhood. My dad had an excellent job in town as the Community School's Transportation Director and was luckily a short drive away if they needed to take me to the doctor. That happened often as my immune system was compromised because of living with Turner syndrome. Even the common cold would turn into ear infections and high fevers. That first year, I put my parents through some major scares and was in and out of the ER many times.

My parents told me that one time I was running such a high fever that my eyes rolled in the back of my head, and I became limp in my dad's arms. My parents rushed me to the ER, and it turned out to be a severe ear infection. By the time I was two, I had so many ear infections that I needed tubes in my ear and would have hearing loss as a result.

My parents begin to see the signs of my disorder within the first year. It took me longer to learn to walk than they hoped, and at times it was a struggle. Luckily though, I did not need those braces the specialist thought I would need and was able to walk normally on my own. This would be the first of many times I would defy the odds in my life. I however soon began to show the signs of delayed motor skills the doctors warned my parents about.

My parents had a specialist visit our home to work on the development of my motor skills. They worked with my hand and eye coordination. I began to show the physical signs of the disorder as I was growing at a below normal rate. That was expected as it was the most common physical feature of those with Turner syndrome. It was clear that medical intervention would someday be needed to achieve a normal adult height. It was also clear that several specialists would be needed throughout my life.

This would be the new normal for our family: frequent visits to specialists throughout most of my childhood and too many trips to the emergency room to count. With all those issues, my parents never lost hope their daughter would have as normal of a life as humanly possible and would make it their number one goal to achieve that. It was not easy, but they wanted the best for their daughter and that would be worth it. With that determination, they began the visits to a referred genetic counselor.

The genetic counselor gave my parents the tools and resources to be advocates for me. They knew what questions to ask each specialist and began to get the full picture of what my limitations may be. They were informed that a series of exams would be needed when I was a little older in order to know the development of my organs and were told that I could have severe hearing loss and vision loss. I visited the counselor regularly for the first few years of my life and learned that I hated needles with a passion.

The first few years of my life, it would become clear that I would face several health challenges. My kidneys were affected, and further tests would be needed at the University of Iowa Children's Hospital to see how much impact the disorder would have on other organs such as my heart. Luckily, my heart was in the normal range, but I would have an increased heart rate for the rest of my life.

With each test result that would come back, my parents would learn to adopt, accept, and chart a new path forward. They would do what was needed to make sure I received the care I needed, even if it were across the state or out of state. The University of Iowa Children's Hospital is a six-hour drive from our home, so a simple test would mean my dad would have to take a least a few days off to make it work. They did this all while keeping our lives as normal as possible.

My mom was even the den mother for my brothers Cub Scout troop, and my dad was active in the community, helping when and wherever he could to make our community better. He would attend and help at local football and baseball games.

He helped volunteer and a drive a local senior citizens' group to community events. To this day, my parents are well respected and admired members of our small-town community. They instilled a passion for community service at an early age, and I will forever be grateful.

The specialist my parents were referred to were wonderful and were always there to answer any questions that my parents would have. Even with all the doctor's visits and tests, I still was an incredibly happy toddler. I was full of energy and talked a mile a minute, and my parents would say I still do. I would ask question all the time and never took no for an answer. I guess you could say I was a precocious child. In fact, one of my earliest words was potassium, and I even used it correctly. My grandma said that when I was two, I told her to eat more bananas as they had potassium in them--like I said, precocious, right?

I had so much energy my parents decided when I turned three to enroll me in dance classes. For a tiny three-year-old, being able to run and dance for a few hours each week was a thrill, and I would do nothing else but dance and want to show anyone who would watch my dance moves.

I do not think they realized just how much enrolling me in those classes would help bring so much happiness to my toddler years.

I made friends that I still have to this day, and it helped me improve my motors skills too. It also gave me the confidence to be on stage, something I would love for most of my childhood. I did ballet, tap, and jazz, and I would play dress up in my recital's costumes and dance around the house for hours. My dad even put a ballet bar in our house so I could practice, and I did for hours as it became an outlet for me to focus on something other than doctors' visits and medicine. It was something to finally look forward to and to feel as though I was just like other kids. For a toddler who was dealt this uncertain disorder, it was important.

By the time I was three, my parents had the routine down to an art form and found the normalcy they wanted when I was first born. My brother was a happy, healthy elementary student, was excelling in school, and was starting little league. I was a happy three-year-old who wanted to do anything and everything. That often scared my parents and sometimes amused them. I was still an extremely sick child, but my parents learned when and when not to visit the doctor. They also learned when something was serious and when it was not. Something that would serve them well in my teen years.

In the next year, my parents and I would prepare for preschool, and I was excited to start preschool. It was a something to look forward to each day and to feel more like a normal child. I began to read, write, and count all the things a normal three-year-old would learn.

That was when my parents could keep me still long enough to work with me. By the time fall hit, I was ready to go to pre-school.

My pre-school teacher was and still is one of the most important people in my life. She has always been my biggest cheerleader. Also, pre-school was when I started to see that I really was a normal kid who went to dance class, acting class, played with kids my own age, and went to birthday parties. It was where I met friends I still have to this day.

Preschool was also where I started to show signs of a nonverbal leaning disability. It was not prevalent, but it was there. My parents would have conversations with my preschool teacher and made the hard decision that it was

11

best to not yet move forward to kindergarten and instead attend preschool again the following year.

My parents worked with me to improve on reading, writing, and my motor skills over the next year. They also wanted to make sure I had time for fun and had time to just be a kid. When an invitation to enter me in the Miss American Princess pageant in early June of 1990 arrived, they decided to enroll me in a child beauty pageant. The winner would get to go to Disney World.My parents thought it would be a terrific way to meet new people and to step out of my shell a little more. When I heard the words Disney World, that was pretty much all I could think about. I mean, what little girl doesn't love Mickey Mouse right?

For three days, I would learn fun dance routines, compete in the talent competition, and be interviewed by a panel of judges. Most importantly, I would spend time with over four hundred girls my own age. It was a blast, and I loved every second of it, especially wearing a formal grown. I felt like Cinderella. My family as well as extended family were there to support me. When it was time for the last finalist to be called, my mom held my hand and said, "You did your best, sweetie, maybe next year." Just as the words came out, my name was called up to the stage and I was a finalist. I was thrilled and of course surprised. With a huge hug from my parents, I headed to the stage.

Each finalist had to tell the judges their name, age and favorite color. When it was my turn, I pulled the mic down as I was about two inches shorter than most the girls, and I quickly introduced myself to the audience and went back in line. Then a few minutes later, they announced 4th to 1st runner up. My name was not called, so I just stayed in line and smiled, just in awe to be a part of it all. Then they said the magic words: "The winner is contestant number eighteen, Nicole Cleveland!"

On June 10, 1990, I was crowned Miss Iowa American Princess 1990. I would be representing the State of Iowa in Tampa, Florida that November, and yes, I was going to Disneyworld.

My mom screamed for joy, and my dad was so thrilled he even dropped the camera. I even got to meet the Governor of Iowa, Terry Branstad. Being chosen as Miss Iowa was an incredibly special moment for this little girl. Not just for the simple reason I was going to Disney World. It meant that the judges had seen me as a normal little girl, and that was the biggest win of all. That November, I went to Tampa and visited Disney World; I got to hug Mickey Mouse and Tigger; and I rode it's a Small World. It was perfect. Although I didn't come home with a national title, I have memories that will last a lifetime.

By the time spring came, it was kindergarten round up time. After meeting with my preschool teacher and the school administrators, it was decided that I was ready to start school. I was so excited about starting school that I picked out my outfit weeks in advance. I still remember it was a jumper with pink and black polka dots, and my mom always had matching bows (it is something my teachers still talk about when they run into me from time to time). I spent the rest of the time talking about starting school nonstop. When fall hit that year, I was more than ready to start this new adventure. I started school in 1991 at Sergeant Bluff-Luton, the same school my dad had attended and now was working in the administration.

Kindergarten was, of course, a transition as it is for all

kids. However, it was much easier than either my parents or I had thought it was going to be. My parents walked me to the classroom, and I just put my backpack in my locker, simply waved, and said, "Bye Mom, bye Dad." I was on my way. I was thrilled to start school and see the friends I had not seen over the summer. I was loving kindergarten except for nap time, something I would later learn to appreciate. Health-wise, I was starting to see more effects of Turner syndrome. An ultrasound of my kidneys would show they were what the doctors said were slightly rotated. This meant that my kidneys kind of looked like the top part of a microphone. This could cause many issues in the future.

I finished kindergarten strong and started the summer with a busy schedule. I was finishing my tenure as Miss Iowa 1990; I would be in parades, do press events, and would travel across the state to crown my successor. I also had a chance to be an extra in a major made-for-TV movie called *A Thousand Heroes*. It was a movie based on a major plane crash in our small Iowa community. I was invited to be a part this movie by the photographer who had taken my pictures over that year.

Over a few weeks, I got to experience what it was like to be on a movie set and visit with the stars of the movie. It is something I will never forget. There was just something that I loved about it. The hustle and bustle of it. Being in a makeup chair every day. Seeing the larger-than-life sets, meeting the amazing actors, and I still see the food service table in my dreams. It was just a once-in-a-lifetime experience for a six-year-old little girl.

Between this dance classes, and my brother in little league, my parents had their hands full, and we seemed to make it work smoothly. We may not have had all the answers, but we had the help of our Lord and Savior. We were learning to navigate the unknown together.

CHAPTER 2

Growing Pains

As I stated earlier, kindergarten was a blast and it was easy to make friends. I took dance classes at Siouxland Movement Arts and acting classes at the children's theater. I was playing soccer with the boys and barbies and swinging on the jungle gyms with the girls. I would often come home with grass stains, to my mom's horror. I was a very well-adjusted little girl. I even had dreams of one day being a professional dancer as an adult. Life would have different plans for me than dancing, but more on that latter.

One physical issue my parents noticed was that I simply stopped growing. My height had not changed since the start of kindergarten, and I was about to enter first grade. This became a concern for my parents. I had not even grown a shoe size since the start of preschool a year before, and I had only grown an inch in a year. I hadn't even outgrown any of my clothes. It was time for medical intervention and to seek a specialist.

During the summer before I entered first grade, it was suggested to my parents by medical staff that I visit a child endourologist to address my complete stop in growth over that year. I had my first visit with Dr. John Sheslo a specialist in children with growth development issues.

He was located at the Sioux Falls Children's Hospital in Sioux Falls, South Dakota, but a few times a week, he would travel to Sioux City. He was an amazing doctor whom I feel ultimately changed my life for the better. I had my first appointment with him in the summer of 1992.

He did several tests to decide what would be the best course of treatment for me. It was suggested that I would start a relatively new treatment program called Human Growth Hormone. This was an injection treatment for children who could not grow without medical intervention. It would consist of six daily injections a week until I would achieve what they would consider a normal adult height. How to determine what my adult height would be, the doctors took the average of both my parents' height to determine my goal height of 5'0. It was suggested I start no earlier than around nine years of age, so for the next two years I would have multiple visits with specialist to decide when and even if should start this therapy.

In the meantime, I was starting to show more struggles in the classroom as well. I was struggling in reading and math. After many visits with teachers and staff, it was decided that I would transfer to the special education program for just these subjects. I would be enrolled in an IEP. This is known as an Individualized Education Program. It would be designed to target my learning struggles and to pinpoint the cause of them as well. In addition to being transferred into special education, I would have weekly therapy sessions with an occupational therapist and a speech therapist. This was recommended so that I could improve my motor skills and my minor speech issues.

When I first started, I was embarrassed, to be honest. I mean, if I needed to be transferred, it meant that I was not as smart as my friends at school. It made me feel again that I was different from my friends when I was deeply trying to fit in. It was an extremely hard adjustment; I would have to leave my classroom and friends in the middle of the morning and my friends would ask, "Where did you go?" I would have to say to a different classroom for reading and my classes. Then the follow up question, *why?* This was a question most any seven-year-old would ask. I would response with hesitation that I needed extra help in math and reading It was a struggle to accept this. Sometimes the hardest part was when my friends at school would have group projects for their reading class; they would have so much fun working as a team, and I felt a little left out because I was not able to take part in it. I would come home often after school crying and just wishing I could be a normal child. I would ask why God would have me go through this. My parents would say, "Sweetie, I want you to understand God doesn't make mistakes. He makes everyone perfect in His own image, and He has a plan for your life. You just have to be strong and patient."

I knew it was going to take me a while to accept my new classes and all the changes that would come from it.

Within a few months I was adjusting well to my new classes. My parents started to see progress. I went from struggling in reading to having a true love of reading. I developed such a love for reading, I seemed to always have book in my hand. My teacher would introduce me to the *Little House on the Prairie* books, and it would open the door to so many adventures. For a girl who was sick a lot, it was a chance to escape and go on these exciting adventures, as well as daydream of a time I could have such an adventure.

It would make me stop dwelling on my health issues or my struggles at school. It also helped me develop my reading skills. It still would take me twice as long as my brother to do homework or to finish assignments in class as my friends as it never came easy to me. It was getting better each day. I went from dreading going to my classes to looking forward to them. It seemed that school was finally back on track, and I was, in my teachers' words, thriving in my new classes.

While adjusting at school, I was starting to get ready for yet another adjustment at home. I was in the second phase of testing for the human growth hormone treatment. That meant that I was in and out of school a lot for the rest of the school year. I had several more test to decide when I would be ready for the final phase of testing. I was one step closer to getting ready to start this life changing treatment.

When summer hit, I was ready to just be a normal kid, no school or doctor appointments. My mom earlier that year went to work full time to help pay for the increasing medical care I would need. My dad had great insurance but still not enough to cover the cost of the injections, which were around $1,900 a month. My mom would work full time at Younkers. With both my parents working, I would spend most of the time on weekdays at my grandparents' house. It made for the most amazing summers. My cousins also spent the weekdays there, so it was so much fun play tag, uno, ball and so much more. My cousin Shana even taught me how to do cartwheels and roundoffs. I loved those summers so much and treasured them and the memories made.

I am still extremely close to my cousins to this day, and we still laugh about our times during those summers.

Now it was time to start back to school as a second-grader, and one of my best friend's moms would be my teacher. I was supper excited because I adore her and still do. Just after school started, my friend became extremely ill, and the tests found it was cancer. It was leukemia. She would be gone for a several months for treatment, so my grades began to be affected. I was trying yet again to adjust to a major change. Not only was my monkey bar partner no longer in school, I also had a new teacher, as her mom would be with her during treatment.

It truly put into prospective that no matter the medical problems I was having, I was still able to be with my friends at school. It made me stop and think just how lucky I was. I prayed for my friend's health daily, and finally towards the end of the school year I got to see my friend back at school and healthy. By the end of the school year, I brought my grades back up, and I even enrolled in a summer rec program. This was summer camp and summer school combined. I was working with teachers in reading, math, crafts, and just having fun being with other kids. It was also a fantastic way to work on my motor skills. By the time third grade would start, I felt I was ready.

Third grade started without a hitch for the most part. I would miss a lot of school for doctor appointments and testing. I was in the final stage of testing for growth hormone treatment. On March 8, 1994, a week before my 9th birthday, the doctors said I was ready to start Human Growth Hormone Therapy. The first thing that I would need to prepare for my injections was the nurse asked me what schedule day off I would like to choose each week.

I had to pick one day a week that I would not have an injection. As the program was for six injections a week,

I picked Friday, as it was usually the night I would have sleepovers with friends after football games and I didn't want my friends to look at me differently. I was worried that if they saw me take the injection, they would look at me like I was sick and fragile. In fact, I never really told anyone but close friends at time that I had Turner syndrome. It was hard for anyone to understand what I was going through because it was so rare, a lot of people didn't even know what it was.

As I said before I hated needles, so my parents had to be creative with injections. I would have my injections at night before bedtime as the doctors recommended. I would try to delay bedtime for long as possible to avoid the injections at first. I was terrified to take them too, but I would take a deep breath and pray and, as it says in Deuteronomy 31:6, "Be strong and courageous. Do not be afraid or terrified because of them, for the LORD your God goes with you; he will never leave you nor forsake you." After a few months, I would get more used to it. My parents even brought was called an injectie. It was a small device that would not show the needle, and it was designed for kids that had to take injections to help them adjust. It did help me for the most part. We were finally getting the new nightly routine down.

At my first checkup, it was showing results already and, to the relief of my parents and me, responding to the medication. That was the news both my parents and I were hoping for. I was starting to grow, and I even needed new shoes. It was worth all the testing and appointments. Just shortly after the check up my parents got an exciting call from our local NBC affiliate in Sioux City, KTIV. They wanted to cast me in a commercial for a local bowling alley in the area to promote the kid's birthday party program they were starting. I was supper excited. I got to eat pizza, bowl, and play mini golf. I even invited a few friends who got to be with me in the commercial; it was such a fun experience and one of the highlights of my childhood.

The commercial aired in the winter of 1994, and it was on for a while. I also continued in pageants until I was around ten. In those five years competing in pageants, I would win over four pageants and would bring home over forty-eight trophies. I got to travel all over the United States by the time I was ten, and I think I had visited over fifteen states. It was exciting time for me. I was doing everything that I loved--dancing, acting, and being with my friends.

I traveled to Disney World, performed in Nashville, Tennessee, was in parades, and was interviewed by the media. I also met some amazing people. They were legends in the entertainment industry such as Richard Thomas, James Colburn, Tiny Tim (just to name a few). I was having experiences that any little girl would dream of.

I knew it was not common to have these experiences, and I soaked up each one of them. My parents always said, "Someday you will look back and realize how extraordinary your childhood was." It certainly was an amazing and uncommon childhood. Even with all the health battles I had to endure, I still was able to enjoy each of these experiences and knew that it wouldn't last forever. I was right, and everything would change when I turned ten.

Shortly after turning ten, my parents set me down to tell me that I would have to give up dance and acting classes, as my medication was so expensive it was no longer in their budget to pay for those classes. I was heartbroken; dancing and acting were my outlets to be a normal kid. It was the place I wasn't separated from the rest of my classmates to attend other classes. It was my way to be creative and express myself and be just a normal ten-year-old little girl, and it was my happy place. Now it was being taken away, and I wasn't sure how to cope with it. Would I ever feel normal again?

I understood why my parents decided to do this. I knew it was a hard decision for them to make. I mean, they had to decide my temporary happiness verses my long-term health needs. Now it was time to find a new outlet for me, and that would take a while to find. I struggled because I was not gifted in sports nor artistic the way my brother was. I also could not play sports due to my health issues. One of the things I did enjoy was singing, so that year I auditioned to take part in the Siouxland Youth Chorus and made it. I was excited to have an outlet again for myself and to be with friends. I also got to travel around the Midwest to perform. We got to perform at Valley Fair amusement park in Minnesota. I made some great friends and loved every second of it.

One day in third grade I was getting a checkup, and they tested my blood sugar levels as at times children who took Human Growth Hormone injections could have elevated levels and increased chances of becoming diabetics. That day they checked it, and my levels were concerning so I had to go in the following week to the Children's Hospital in Sioux Falls for testing to see if I would need to be classified as a diabetic or if it was just a small elevation and would need repeated testing while on the injection program.

The week before testing was full of anxiety for myself and my parents. I was terrified that I would need to have more medication and a controlled diet. Worse, I would need yet another injection each day, and with this there were no days off. To add to the anxiety, my dad had recently been diagnosed as a diabetic at the age of forty-five, both my grandmas had it, and my grandfather who was extremely ill at this time also had it. It felt it almost certain I would likely have it given my family history.

Now it was officially the test day. We would know for sure after today what our next step would be. The test would be that I was to get inserted with an IV (yay, more needles, did I say I hated needles?). The icing on the cake for the already stressful day was that it took the nurse three tries with the IV for it to work. Now after that I would drink this extremely sweet drink multiple times throughout the day. When I mean sweet, it was like just dinking a whole bottle of maple syrup. Throughout the day they were test my blood levels

After several hours, the doctor called my parents and me back to discuss my test. To our relief, although I had elevated blood sugar levels, it was not enough to have a cause for concern, and I would continue my current course of treatment. I had to be tested several times while I continued to take the injections. It was the result that we had been praying for because the injections and the current course of treatment were working wonders.

When I say wonders, I mean exactly that. When I first started the injections, I was at a standstill; I literally stopped growing. I was only 3'6" when I started. Without the course of treatment, I would likely not have grown to even reach four feet. By the end of the first year, I was 3'11". That may not seem like a big jump, but from someone who hadn't grown in over a year it was a milestone. It was the first time I had outgrown my shoes in over two years.

By the time I started fourth grade, I would reach the milestone of four feet that the doctors said would have been my adult height without treatment. I remember how excited I was when I reached it. For a main reason, I could ride the adult rides at the amusement parks.

Not only did I reach a milestone in my health journey, I also reached a milestone in school too. I was really starting to see progress in the classroom; I was really starting to enjoy my math and reading classes. I also no longer needed speech or occupational therapy. Although I still struggled with it and homework did take me longer than most, it was getting better. I was also finally diagnosed with what is called a nonverbal learning disability. What this meant was that my disability was not language based. It was mostly motor skills based. This would help my parents and teachers pinpoint the best way to approach and handle my education going forward. Non-learning disabilities are extremely common in girls that have Turner syndrome, and since most are not diagnosed until they are in their teens due to its rareness, it is often a silent struggle for most.

As you know, I was luckily diagnosed shortly after birth, so I was blessed to have timely access to treatment and education programs that were maybe not available to those without the diagnosis. Although at the time I didn't feel that lucky, like when I had to give up dance, but looking back at this time I was extremely blessed, and it was those experiences and challenges that were shaping who I was becoming. It would give me more empathy for others and a desire to help those who struggle like I did.

I was also getting ready to have yet another change: I was getting braces. After a few years of appointments with an orthodontist, it was decided that I would need braces. I was not excited; for one I was a short, and to be honest, I was getting teased already for being short. Adding braces to that mix was not something I wasn't extremely thrilled to be doing. In December of fourth grade, I got them put on and to my surprise wasn't getting teased for it much. I started to have a lot of fun with it. Each month that I would go in for my adjustments and cleaning, I got to pick out colored rubber bands to put on my braces. I would pick red and pink in February for Valentine's Day or two greens for Saint Patrick's Day. I was getting used to it.

As I was in my finale year of elementary school, I was figuring out how to learn, grow, and adapt to each new challenge that I met. I was starting to show who I was more and more and realized that Turner syndrome did not define me. I was more than this disorder. Not to say I didn't have those days--believe me, I did have those days.

Days I didn't want to go to school because I would get teased for my height, or it was a test day, and I never did well on test.

As I was approaching middle school I was coming into my own and those experiences and challenges were making me who I was and who I would become. It was something to not be ashamed of; it was just a part of growing up. I just had simply more growing pains

CHAPTER 3

Charting a New Path Forward

Starting middle school is hard to navigate; it is like a jungle and finding your compass to navigate those halls can be a bit of a challenge. Add braces, being short, and the worst wave in history, and you're starting school at the bottom of the food chain.

Trying to learn to navigate those halls would take a while, but soon I would find my way.

I was teased mostly for my height, and it was usually daily. It would be from friends, classmates, even a teacher. It is still something that I battle with daily. I learned to take it in stride. One day after school, I was watching an episode of *Full House*. You know, the episode where Stephanie gets glasses and is having a challenging time being teased by classmates. In that episode, Urkel tells her to crack a joke about it, and soon they will know it doesn't bother you and that you can laugh at yourself.[1]

It was like a lightbulb clicked on, and I was like, *Of course I may never be tall, but I can show my friends that I am okay with it.* I learned that I was a child of God, and I knew that as long as I carried Him with me, He would see me through and I would be okay. I have learned this has served me well as an adult too.

Being teased is never easy, and believe me, I still struggle with it to this day and likely always will. I learned to accept the things I cannot change and have the courage to stand up for myself when needed.

Middle school certainly started off rocky, as it does for most tweens, but it was also in middle school that I came out of my shell and started to show my friends a little more of who I was. I adapted to new classes well too, and I loved social studies and history the most. Being in special education was easier too because all students rotated classrooms, so I no longer stood out from my classmates.

It was also in middle school I discovered a new passion, something I had been trying to find since giving up dance class a year before. I started to love politics and would often stay up past my bedtime to listen to the news and current political affairs. I know this wasn't very normal for an eleven-year-old girl, but I found it to be remarkably interesting. It was also something that my dad and I bonded over. We loved talking politics at supper, and he would always have great insight into current events. This was becoming a new passion and something I found extremely interesting. I love watching the debates and would often wish I was there asking the politicians questions. I just loved everything about it, and over the years my passion for this would only grow.

I also continued to use music as an outlet and joined the middle school choir. It was chance for me to step out of my comfort zone, and I even sang a solo at the school program. I looked forward to this class period each day and would practice at night after school. It boosted my self-confidence, which was something that I struggled with in middle school and to be honest still do.

What also helped my self-confidence was it was now time to get those braces off--one step closer to looking like a normal girl. I was thrilled and not only because I could finally eat popcorn (my favorite). I would start off sixth grade without braces, a fantastic way to start the school year. I had also grown a few inches over that year, so it was the first year in a long time that I started school feeling confident.

Sixth grade was pretty much standard for the most part. I was doing good in school, getting good grades, and had great friends. One day as I was walking home from school a friend of mine showed me a poster that invited kids to join the Mayor's Youth Commission. He stopped and said, "Hey Nicole, that seems to be perfect for you, I know how you like politics." The sign said this was a volunteer organization for kids in junior high and high school to help bring activities and youth events to community. I applied a few days later and It took a few weeks to hear anything. Around a month later, I would get a call from the mayor of our community, and I would be interviewed for an opened spot on the commission. It was a tough interview and a little nerve racking as the mayor himself was doing the interview. After a few moments into the I interview, I felt more at ease. I left feeling surprisingly good about the interview.

About a month after the interview, I got a letter in the mail, and it said I was invited to be a member of the Sergeant Bluff Mayor's Youth Commission. I was thrilled; it was a chance for me to even more involved in my community and to make a difference. The first meeting would be the following month, and we started off with a bang. The first major project we did was designing and installing new community signs as our old ones were in bad shape. The signs turned out nice; they were yellow and green, shaped like the state of Iowa, and said simply, "Welcome to Sergeant Bluff."

They are still in great shape today.

Mayors' Youth Commission gave me a great understanding of community service and the ins and outs of city government. At the end of the year, since we were funded by the city, we had to present our plans and programs to the city council each year to get funding and to request an increase in the funding if needed. I learn to be more comfortable with public speaking the more I got involved with the commission.

With sixth grade ending, it was time to focus on summer plans, and for me I would spend most of this trying to convince my mom to let me cut and highlight my hair. I wanted to look like "more like an adult." I finally at the end of the summer cut my hair and highlighted. This was my first real drastic hair change since I was a little girl. I had always had perms, and as a little girl it was cute, but when I was a teenager looking like a little girl, it was last thing I wanted to be told. With that and new Tommy Hilfiger jeans thanks to the Younkers discount, my mom had it felt like I was truly ready to start junior high.

The start of seventh grade was a challenge; I was starting wood shop and as I stated earlier, I was not the artistic person in my family. Let's say that wood shop was not my best subject, and I would never be a carpenter. I did manage to pull together a pretty good-looking clock but that was about it. I was ready to move on to cooking class—that, I enjoyed.

In the middle of seventh grade my friends and I decided to try out for cheerleading for the following year. I was hesitating at first as I wasn't sure I was good enough to make the squad. That spring was tryouts. During tryouts, we were taught three cheers and the school fight song cheer. Later we would perform it in front of the judges and the coaches. We would also have to perform a cheer jump or stunt.

My turn came, and I was one of the last to tryout, so everyone was telling me their experiences. I was ready, but as each of my friends approached me stating how nerve racking it was, I was starting to fear walking into the gym to do my tryout. After about an hour wait, my number was called, and I did my tryout. I breezed through the cheers and school song. I then performed a roundoff, thankful that my cousin taught it to me.

After tryouts were completed the waiting game started. The coach said later that night the list of who made it would be on the front doors of the school. Around eight that evening my mom drove me over to the school, and I walked to the front door. There it was, my name. I was going to be a basketball cheerleader the following year, and I was so excited even my cousin was going to be on the team, so it was for sure going to be a great season. I hugged my cousin, ran to the car, and yelled I made the team.

It may seem to some who read this that making the squad isn't really that big of a deal; cheerleading is just an easy sport, and millions make the squads each year.

For me, the excitement was more than just making the team; it was about being accepted and included by my classmates. I was now just one of the girls and would get to share those important school moments with my friends. I was finally part of a team and as said in Thessalonians 5:11 "therefore encourage one another and build each other up, just as in fact you are doing." For me, being a cheerleader was that milestone moment so many who have Turner syndrome or any genetic disorder understand.

It is that moment you strive for or wish for but so many times the barriers of the disorder can limit you or sometimes make it extremely hard to achieve. When you do achieve the goal, it is even sweeter and more impactful than one can imagine. It is a chance to be a part of a team and to have that support system to lean on each other and support one another.

I finished seventh grade on a strong note, making both choir and cheerleading, and my grades and progress in school were also on track. I was ready for my final year of middle school. Eighth grade started off busy, and I soon would find out that this was just the start of my busy schedule for the rest of my school career. I would get to school by 7 a.m. for cheerleading practice then to school; then after school, often I would work with my choir director. Then it was home to homework or often a follow up doctor's appointments When I did have free time and mine was extremely limited it was spent with friends.

I loved my last year of junior high and my classes. I was traveling a lot with my cheerleading squad and got to even be in the high school homecoming parade, which was a lot of fun and rewarding. I was making new friends and was feeling included. I was asked to the school dances, went shopping with the girls, and just felt like a normal teenager, and it was getting less and less often that I would be thinking about my health battles. In fact, I was feeling surprisingly good and having enormous success with the human growth hormone treatment too. I was reaching the goals my doctors hoped I would. God was blessing me in ways only He could and supplying me lessons only He could.

Although I still struggled a little with math and reading, I was making great strides in those areas and was really making progress, so much so that it was said in my IEP that I was above the benchmarks that they had set for me. This was something that my parents and myself had been working toward since I was first transferred into the special education program in the second grade.

I was also learning to be an advocate for myself. At the doctors' appointments, my parents were slowly starting to let me take the lead and ask questions and address my own health issues. They did feel that I was fourteen and that I should start to lead the conversations related to my health. That certainly did not mean that I was making my own health decisions, it just meant that I was starting to have more input on my health and treatments. My parents had always included me in the conversations since I was a child, but they always made the decisions. Now I wasn't just being included, I now had input in it.

This has served in well in my adult life as I navigate my health journey.

Not only was I being an advocate for my own health choices, I was also learning how to be my own advocate in the classroom. It was paying off too. One spring day after school I had a letter from an organization called Quota Club International. I was nominated by my teachers to be awarded the Siouxland Quota Club Award. This is for the student who has achieved excellence and the most progress in the classroom over her middle school career.

I was stunned. I knew I was achieving good grades and personally felt that I was progressing, but this was something I wasn't thinking or even knew I was up for. When it came in the mail, I suddenly felt overwhelmed with emotion. School was never the easiest for me and to be honored by my teachers meant that I was getting closer to those goals that I had set for myself.

A few weeks later my parents and I would attend the annual Quota Club Luncheon where I would be honored and receive my award. It was a full circle moment for me. In second grade I was scared and embarrassed to start special education. Now, I was a teenager getting ready to head into high school feeling prepared and relieved that I did accomplish and face some of those challenges my parents and I were unsure I would be able to do.

It was finally the last day of junior high and my friends and I were all getting ready for the eighth grade graduation. It was important; even friends of mine had their parents rent a limo for the afternoon. I was simply happy to have a nice lunch and not eat the school lunch for the day. Towards the end of the day, I walked into our middle school gym. I saw my parents smile, and it was going to be a special moment for them. As awards were being called, I was thinking I would not be getting more then the middle school diploma.

I was awarded one for choir and for being a part of the middle school paper called the Arrow and cheerleading. It was now time to award the final award. The award was presented to two students in the entire grade. This award was called the SBLEA Award. It was short for what is known as the Sergeant Bluff Luton Education Association. This award was given to the two students who carried out and demonstrated the goals of the association.

I was certain that my name would not be called. I was a student who was in special education and still struggled at times in school. Granted I was making a large amount of progress, but I still felt that I had a long way to go before I achieved anything close to this type of honor.

Then our principal called the name of a classmate, then the principal called my name. I was stunned and looked over at my parents seated in the bleachers and saw them smile with pride. It really happened; all the hard work my parents and I went through to get to this point. The long hours spent helping me understand the homework, the uncertainty if they made the right decision, it all led to this point. It was more than just an award; it was the validation that the decisions made were paying off and that regardless of the struggles I was going to be okay. It was a comfort for my parents to know that the daughter that was born with so much uncertainty and so many possible limitations was not just doing okay in school but was now, according to the very staff that are most involved in her education, successful.

As a teenager, starting out with braces, unruly hair, and short stature meant adding to normal everyday teenage challenges. As I was about to leave the hollow halls of SBL middle school, I was starting to see myself the way my friends and family seen me. I was using my voice for community service and to be my own advocate. I was facing my fears of being judged and tried out for the cheerleading squad and made it. I even put myself out there and performed a solo at the spring concert. I come into middle school unsure of what my future would hold and if I would be successful in the classroom to thriving in and out of the classroom.

Now this didn't mean that I didn't struggle and that I was not unsure of myself. It just met that I felt I was ready to head into high school I could start to dream and carve out a future for myself. It meant that I should stop putting so many limitations on myself and to set new goals, even the goals that seemed too lofty or unrealistic. I had put my trust in God, and all though I didn't always understand His ways, I knew that He had a purpose and a plan for my life. It was time for high school and to chart a new path forward for myself.

CHAPTER 4

Accepting Life's Curve Balls

I thought by the time I started high school I was prepared for the unexpected because I had been thrown so many diverse types of curve balls that I was certain nothing could surprise me. I thought high school could not be that different from finishing middle school for me. After all, the classmates I was entering high school with were the same kids I had gone through elementary and junior high school with.

I was mistaken; it was a whole new adjustment and I had to learn the value of time management, something that can often be a challenge for those who suffer from nonverbal learning disabilities. Juggling between school, friends, starting a part time job, and all the extracurricular programs I was involved in, I was often so busy that I never really appreciated how far I had come since I was diagnosed.

I was focusing on being normal teenage girl and not on my limitations. I was in cheerleading, which I loved. I was a JV football cheerleader, so I was usually spending Monday nights at the football field. I also tried out for our school's choir groups called LOVE and 75th St. Jazz (LOVE stood for Ladies of Vocal Excellence). I made both, and as someone who used music as an outlet and to feel accepted, it was validation. I remember coming home after school and telling my mom I made LOVE. The look on my mom's face was one of horror. I couldn't stop laughing when I told her what LOVE really was.

I was also involved in Mayor's Youth Commission, something that I had been in for almost three years, and it kept me busy with events. I thoroughly enjoyed the start of high school, and my biggest worries were basically normal teenage girl things. *Does the boy in my science class notice me? Will I get my homework done in time to go to the movie with my friends?* Like I said, your basic teenage things. The only difference was I also had worries of my health and visits to the doctor were still common. I never really thought about anything else. I was simply just too busy to stop and think about them.

All that changed on the morning of 09/11/01. Like many of you it started off as a normal day. I was getting ready for school when I turned on the *Today Show* when I saw that a plane had just crashed into the World Trade Center. I, like many of you, at first thought this had just been a horrible plane crash. What I saw next was something I will never forget. While live on the air, I saw the second tower get hit. With tears in my eyes, I said a prayer and went to school scared, knowing this was now not a horrible plane crash but a terrorist attack.

I walked into my P.E class that morning; my classmates were as terrified and angry as I was. Our teacher knowing this told us all to take a seat on the bleachers and simply told us to pray. As I left my first class that day and walked down the hallways all I saw were classmates and teachers watching the TV. As I approached my classroom, I heard my teacher say, "Oh no, not again." I looked up to the TV and saw that a plane had just crashed into the Pentagon. It was for certain we were seeing my generation's Peral Harbor, and I would see friends and family sent off to war. To heighten the fear of uncertainty, the sound of jet planes taking off from the nearby airbase made as all stop in our tracks. We knew this was not a normal training exercise; they were preparing for war. In the days that followed my cousin was sent to Ground Zero to help with recovery, and it was certain the events of 9/11/01 would change my view of the world. We were suddenly no longer as carefree as we all were just few days before.

I wrestled with trying to understand why God would allow such a tragedy to happen. I then was reminded by Romans 8:28: "And we know that all that happens to us is working for our good if we love God and are fitting into his plans." I may not know or understand the reasons, but I knew I loved God and He had never failed me. He may have not always given me the answer I wanted, but He always gave the answer I needed.

Even with the uncertainty of the world, our teachers tried to make sure our routine was as normal as possible with getting us back into practice and just trying to make school a safe place for all of us. My classmates and friends all handled it in diverse ways. For myself, I turned to music as it was and always had been a source of comfort for me. For others, they attended their football and volleyball practices as it was their way, just like music was for me, to find a since of normalcy and to process what was happening in the world around us.

Though the world might have been in turmoil, I was still managing to do well in school and even getting above average grades. There were even talks that I may someday soon be transferred out of special education. Though I still had a way to go before I could get transferred. It was a rewarding feeling to know that I was making strong progress in the classroom and that my challenging work was making a difference.

I was not only making progress in the classroom, I was also making progress on the health front too. I reached my goal height of 5'1". This was a milestone and something I never thought I would reach. A few weeks later, it was recommended that I stop human growth hormone treatment injections. This was a bittersweet time for me as I was extremely ready to no longer take the nightly injections, but it also meant that I would have to say goodbye to the medical staff who helped me throughout my treatment. This was hard for me as they had been there for throughout this process and had become almost like an extended family. For almost nine years I had made monthly trips to see them. I had gotten to know them well and appreciated their support throughout these challenging treatments.

With the successes in school and my health I was starting to dream that I could achieve more than what was laid out for me. That I needed to stop putting so many barriers up and be more open to new possibilities. I needed to stop saying, *Because I had Turner syndrome, I could not do this*, and start saying, *Why not at go for it?* This may sound so easy for some; just simply saying go for it was easier said than done. For me, this was something that I struggled with. I always seemed to doubt my abilities because I had struggled both with Turner syndrome and my learning disability. I had grown more confident over the years but still had barriers on myself thinking those big goals are just too far out of reach for me. Now I had to work on saying I can instead of I can't. As it says in Philippians 4:13 "I can do all things through Christ who strengthens me."

This was put to the test when my teacher asked me to share my story about living with Turner syndrome for a school project. The project was on children with genetic disorder and one of the disorders in the book we were discussing was Turner syndrome. She asked me if I would be willing to share with classmates that I had Turner syndrome and how it affected me. I was completely terrified if I was honest, it was the first time many of my classmates and friends would learn that I even had Turner syndrome.

I never shared it with many people. I just never thought my friends would understand the complexity of the disorder. I looked like an regular teenage girl, just shorter than average. I just thought no one would understand the health issues I faced with this disorder after all it was so rare, I was the only I knew who was diagnosed with this so how could I expect anyone to know or understand anything about this disorder.

With those thoughts, I now had to prepare to tell my story to classmates and answer any questions they would have. As I walked up to the front of the class, I had a million thoughts racing through my head. The main though was, *How will my friends and classmates react? Will it change how they look at me and think of me?* I was soon going to find out. I started off by explaining what Turner syndrome was and how it was diagnosed.

I then began the process of telling my story for the first time to classmates. I opened up to them and began sharing how I was diagnosed my struggles with Turner syndrome. I even laid out my learning disabilities. As I continued to speak, I became more at ease. I had been worried for so long about it that I never really realized just how therapeutic it would be to share my story. I came to the realization that by sharing my struggles with this disorder I would no longer be alone, that my friends were now on this journey with me.

After I was done sharing my story and information on this disorder, my friend stopped me in the hall after class and asked me, "Why haven't you ever told me about this?" Honestly, I didn't really understand myself. It wasn't that I was ashamed of having this. I learned to accept it a long time ago. It was more not wanting to stand out and feel different from my friends. I wanted to be included not excluded, and my not sharing my struggles with this I avoided being excluded. I thought it was best to do so.

After sharing this with classmates, I found my worries were completely unfounded. I was asked questions but for the most part my friends and classmates treated me the same. They didn't exclude me or worse treat me with pity. I certainly didn't feel sorry for myself, so I didn't want my friends to feel sorry for me either. I found that if my friends and classmates didn't see me differently then I was able to share my story more and no longer feel that I needed to keep this disorder to myself. It was the first step in sharing my story with others, and by doing so I would start to bring awareness to this rare disorder.

While some teachers encouraged me to share my story and encouraged me in this process, one teacher discouraged me to strive for, as she would say, "unrealistic expectations or goals." One day while I was in class, we had a college admissions advisor give a talk on the college application process and what to expect. I was only a sophomore at this point; however, it was never too early to start thinking about my future. After the speaker left, my friends and I started talking about all the colleges we wanted to apply to and what we might major in. We were just being normal sixteen-year kids excited about the future.

I was more excited than most as even being able to talk about college was a milestone for me. Being able to share and dream about college with my friends was the full circle moment. That moment would be short lived. Shortly after class we were headed out and my teacher asked me to stay after class a second. I was unsure what this could possibly be about; I had just gotten a good report from this very teacher. As I approached her desk, she asked me to follow her into the other room so we could talk. As I took a seat, she started off the saying, "I see that you and your friends were talking about attending college and that you had plans to attend yourself."

I replied, "Yes, I am and looking forward to it soon."

She had this concerned look on her face that only meant what she was going to say to me next was not going to be good. I was right. She said, "Nicole, you need to understand going to a four-year college is not an option for someone like you with your learning disability."

At first, it caught me off guard.

I was trying to absorb what was just said.

How could a teacher say this to a student? Shouldn't they encourage you to strive for such a goal?

After a few moments, I finally was able to speak. I simply asked, "Why?"

She said I would not be able to handle the courses and that I would likely fail. I was almost brought to tears by this comment. It was so hard to grasp that any teacher would talk to a student like this, and how many had she spoken to in this way before? I replied, "I don't understand why. I have a 3.0 grade point average; I even currently have an A in your class and have never been late on any assignments. When have I given you any reason to doubt college is an option?"

She replied, "I have had a number of students who have been successful in high school, but they often have unrealistic expectations and I see this in you."

I simply just said I understood and walked out the classroom. I was devastated, and as I walked to my next class, I started to cry. Just when I thought I was making so much progress in school and that I could make goals like so many of my friends. Now I was told to basically stop daydreaming and to focus on realistic dreams. As I was walking, I stopped by the school counselor's office thinking I could ask him for his input. I relayed to him what the teacher had just told me.

He said, "Nicole, you should have never had to experience this. No teacher should tell a student that. I see your grades, and you are currently sitting at the top half of your class. You are involved in several activities. Any college would be happy to have you as a student."

I again started to cry and just felt like this day was one of the worst in my school career. I had come so far and finally stopped doubting myself and felt like my goals were finally in reach, only to have the rug pulled out from under me. All the demanding work I put forward seemed to be for nothing.

That night I talked to my parents about what had happened that day, and they were in as much shock as I was and honestly somewhat angry. I asked them if they thought I should give up on college. They said that I had worked too hard to let someone put limitations on me and only I could decide what was best for my future.

I went to bed that night not able to get the day's events out of my head, and the words she said just kept replaying. After a while, I said to myself, "Okay, Nicole, you were told you were not going to be able to walk normal and you are. You overcome health struggles and come out of each of them stronger, so what makes you think college would be any different?" I woke up determined to never let anyone tell me I was not going to be able to achieve my goals. I needed to not let anyone hold me back from my dreams. As I always did, I looked to God for answers and could not get the verse of Psalm 27:10 out of my head "The LORD is the stronghold of my life-- of whom shall I be afraid? When evil men advance against me to devour my flesh, when my enemies and my foes attack me, they will stumble and fall. Though an army besiege me, my heart will not fear; though war break out against me, even then will I be confident."

With this new determination, I made it my goal to stay the course and when the time was right, I would apply to college. Frankly, I couldn't wait to show that teacher my acceptance letter when the time was right. First though, I needed to work on being transferred out of the Special Education Program. It wasn't that I was ashamed of being in special education, in fact I think it was the largest reason for me being able to grow and be successful in school. I wanted to be transferred out in large part I just wanted to have a fresh start. I wanted to move on from this, and I certainly learned the power of being able to stand up and what being my own advocate really meant.

This would not be easy, as my health would also complicate this further. I was still having several ear infections, so I was referred to an ENT doctor. He did test, and it showed that I had a large hole in my ear drum, and it would need to be repaired. A few weeks later I was taken into surgery to repair the hole, and it was successful but would have even more hearing loss because of it.

When this was fixed and my health was back on track the following year, I worked nonstop and challenged myself more. I was determined to achieve my goal of being out of special education by the end of my sophomore year, and I achieved that goal. Now I would still have an IEP, but it would be revised and less detailed as I had reached many of the goals my IEP was designed for.

As I entered my junior year of high school I was in regular math and English courses for the first time since second grade of elementary school. After being told I wouldn't be able to handle the workload, I now was going to either prove myself or the others right. I am happy to say although it was at times a challenge, I was rising to meet them.

I was still getting above average grades and keeping up with the extracurricular activities that I was involved in. The doubt I still had about attending college was starting to subside, and I was starting to do college visits and getting ready to start the application process. Now I needed to start thinking about what I possibly wanted to major in after high school. I, like most of my friends, was undecided.

That would change the summer before my senior year.

A few months before the end of my junior year our local American Legion was accepting applications to attend Girl's State. Now you may be asking, *what is Girl's State?* It is a weeklong program that teaches the inner workings of state government. When I saw the announcement at school, I knew I had to apply. A few weeks later I had my interview with legion members. Shortly after the interview, I was chosen to attend this weeklong program. It would be held at Iowa State University the following June.

When the end of June hit, I was ready but had no idea how this program would inspire me. I learned how the inner workings of our state government. I also learned how to campaign and run for elective office. I even campaigned and ran for Girls State Senate and won. On the last day of Girls State, we would meet and draft a bill to be sent to our state Governor to review. It was an amazing week, and I left knowing what to major in college. I was going to major in Political Science. I also knew I wanted to get more involved in politics.

Later that summer, I started looking at what campaigns I wanted to get involved in, and after 9/11, foreign policy was one of my top concerns. With that, I volunteered for President George W. Bush's reelection campaign and would meet the first lady, Vice President Cheney, and his wife Lynn, as well as many other national and local leaders.

Over that year before college, I knew political science was my calling, the only questions were *can I do it* and *what school would feel the needs and experiences I was looking for*. I, of course, wanted to stay in Iowa because outside of Washington DC, it is pretty much the place to be if you're a politico. I also wanted to stay close by due to my medical needs, and starting college was a big enough adjustment. Adding new doctors would be even more stressful. I decided to go on a campus visit to Morningside College, now a university, to visit with the political science department members and professors, and to get a tour. I grew up only fifteen minutes from this campus but being on campus felt like a whole new experience, and it just felt right.

That winter I applied to a few colleges but did have my heart set on going to Morningside. That early spring, I got acceptance letters from other colleges but still hadn't heard from Morningside. I was getting concerned that my dream was just that, a dream. Maybe my teacher was right; I needed to rethink college. After about a few more weeks of no more response, my mom and dad called me out of school and in the front seat sitting there was a large envelope from Morningside College. My mom handed me the envelope, and it said those words I have been waiting for: "Congratulations, Nicole, it is with immense pleasure that I inform you of your acceptance to Morningside College for the fall semester of 2004."

I started to cry; it was just overwhelming news. I had worked so hard and had so much to overcome that this letter never seemed possible. Even my teacher was saying the same thing, so I always had doubts. When I read the letter, those doubts became a distant memory. I was now going to college. I was extremely grateful and knew the power of prayer could move mountains.It was now time to start planning the next chapter.

With all the excitement of senior year and the joy of the future there were also a lot of last moments. The last high school homecoming, prom, and choir performance--all the last were happening at a rapid pace and with each event, we were inching closer to one of the most important days of anyone's life : high school graduation.

On May 23rd, 2004, I officially walked the halls of Sergeant Bluff Luton High School as a student for the final time and said goodbye to my friends as we celebrated this milestone. We talked about our future, our goals, and it seemed like our future was planned out, we just had to get there. We did achieve most of our goals and some we didn't even know we had. We learned to lean on God more than ever, in particularly the words of Proverbs 3:5:6: "Trust in the lord with all your heart and lean not on your own understanding in all own your ways submit to him and he will make your paths straight."

We also never thought about all the curve balls along the way.

CHAPTER 5

Lifelong Learning

The few months that followed high school went extremely fast. I spent the summer before college spending time with friends as much as possible and volunteering with President Bush's Reelection campaign. I also got to meet during this time the Vice President of the United States and greet him upon arriving on Air Force 2. It was certainly an eventful summer, and then it was time to head off to college at Morningside.

I was ready for this new chapter and determined to be successful, but I also tried to enjoy as much of the college experience as I could. I started off with a challenging course load. The first week I finished classes I said to my mom, "I am not sure I am going to be able to handle it. Maybe my teacher was right."

After a few beats, I said, "No, Mom, I am going to rise to the challenge. I have had so many people thinking this would not be possible. I am going to prove them wrong. God never gives you more than you can handle, and I am not going to give up or fail by lack of trying."

With that said, I was one of those college kids in the campus library always with a book in her hand, but I made sure I took time for breaks and friends.

I also wanted to get more involved on campus too. I was in several campus organizations the start of my first year. Some of them were Morningside Activities Council, College Republicans, Morningside Civic Union, and other organizations as well. I was embracing and soaking in all that college had to offer, and I was staying on top of my studies as well. I finished my first semester strong, all A's and B's. Most importantly, I felt at home and like I made the right decision on attending Morningside. Some of my friends who were attending other colleges were often home sick and having a tough time adjusting. For me, it was a smooth adjustment. Granted I was home every night, however the college experience so far was the one I had always dreamed of. Not to say it was perfect, but it was certainly perfect place for me.

Second semester, I was approached about attending a May Term in Washington DC. May term was a mouth long class in May that was usually traveling to points of intertest around the globe. For me, the politico Washington DC was the epic destination and one I have never been to and dreamed of going. That May, a group of us went with our Political Science professor to DC. This was my first time ever flying.

Now you might be asking how someone who has traveled to over fifteen states, *How can you not have been on a plane?* The answer: my family traveled everywhere by car. We may have put on thousands of miles, but we made great memories that I will treasure always.

DC did not disappoint. We got a tour of the U.S. Capitol and visit with our U.S. senator, Chuck Grassley. We visited several Smithsonian museums and national monuments. We spent the time learning the ins and outs of federal government. We even got to be inside the Supreme Court to hear oral arguments. I got to see up close Sandra Day O'Conner, the first women to ever serve on the Supreme Court. A few weeks later, she announced her retirement from the bench. We also had to interview for an internship. I interviewed with the Republican National Committee. I was too young for the internship, but it was a chance for me to prepare for what a DC internship would be like. I was only in DC for a week but knew someday I would want to comeback.

The next month I started my summer with amazing opportunity to intern for Senator Grassley in Sioux City's district office. I had applied and was interviewed in early spring and was offered the internship shortly after. My first day was full of nerves and excitement. I was thrilled to be given this opportunity but knew that I also had to prove myself. I was a first-year student yet in college, so I knew I was young, but they took a chance on me anyway, so I did not want to let them down. For the next two months, I would learn not just about the current pieces of legislation that were being debated but the amazing work the senate offices do for citizens in their state. From helping a veteran get the medical care he needs to helping with international adoptions, each day they are making an impact on people's lives, and this often gets overlooked in the heat of campaigning. I leaned so much, and shortly after that I officially declared political science as my major. I knew I wanted to make a positive impact on people's lives, and seeing what the senator's office did each day, I knew I wanted to do the same someday as well.

I finished my internship a few weeks before heading back to start my sophomore year of college just as my friends were getting ready to head back to their college campuses, so we made the most of the time we had left and sharing stories of our first-year adventures. Now it was time to get back to campus myself and prepare for the start of sophomore year. I also was ready to start challenging myself more and be opened to new possibilities. I would only have the college experience once, so why wouldn't I make the most of it? In addition to the programs I was in, I also joined the college radio station KMSC and was given the opportunity to even cohost my own political talk show. I would debate from the Republican standpoint, and my friend would take on the Democrat standpoint. We would do this every week, and it was such a fun and informative experience. I even had the chance to interview local and national politicians as they came to campus.

During that year, I also joined the Mock Trial Team. It is exactly as it sounds. We would get a trail case and would prepare both sides. Then when we were ready would enter competitions around the country. I got to compete at the university of Kansas, Harvard, and UCLA as well as many regional colleges too. It was a wonderful time, and some of my best friends from college were the ones I made during my time in mock trial. I even got to see parts of the country I had never seen before. I was truly soaking in God's beauty as I traveled across our great nation.

I was enjoying every moment of my college experience, not to say there weren't any struggles along the way. My dad and mom were each battling health issues of their own. My dad had triple bypass surgery and my mom was dealing with several medical issues, so I was feeling the added stress of worrying about their health. Trying to stay focused on class was a challenge because I was always worrying when the next medical crisis would happen with them or my extremely ill grandfather. When they would go in for further testing, I would always be afraid of the outcome, concerned that we would face the worst. I began to understand the worry my parents must have faced dealing with all my health issues. It was now my turn to be on the other side of the worry. I would lean on the words of Psalm 56:3, which says, "When I am afraid, I put my trust in you." I needed to be reminded of that during this time more the ever.

My dad's bypass was successful, and he was back to working and feeling better. Mom was still battling back and lung issues but as always tried to stay positive and manage the pain as much as possible. Even with the concerns I faced at home, I still managed to keep up my grades and my involvement in the organizations on campus. I kept up a 3.0 GPA and was promoted to promotions director of our college radio station. I was making news promos, helping with programming, and working with other organizations on campus to help promote their events.

I did this all while holding down three part time jobs through college to help pay my way. Now I still took out student loans. Private colleges were expensive, but I was blessed with great scholarships and grants that did help with the cost There was rarely a day that I either wasn't working or had a meeting, but on days I was free, I soaked up my free time as much as I could. I spent it with my friends and even went on a road trip with some of my closet college friends to Wisconsin for spring break. Now sophomore year was coming to end, and I had yet to pick a minor. I was so focused on political science that I had never looked for other interests.

Then, as I was finishing my radio program for the year, I was called in to my professor's office. He asked me if I decided on a minor yet. I said, "No, I haven't."

He laughed, "Nicole, I think you did without even realizing it. You have enough credits to declare a second major in journalism." I was surprised but it dawned on me all my electives seemed to be commutation courses. I would start off my junior year double majoring in political science and journalism. I was ready for the exciting challenge, but more importantly, it felt like this was a huge validation that not only was I doing well in college, I was able to be successful enough to take on a second major. I was again defying the odds and expectations that so many people had set for me. I knew it would be a challenge, but it was one I was ready to embrace. I knew God was in control, and He was guiding me.

The start of my junior year, I was as busy as ever. I was chosen to be the news director of my college radio station and was elected to serve on Student Government. Not to mention I was also elected to be the vice president of Morningside College Civic Union. I certainly had myself spread thin, but it would prepare me for the future. I had a large class load too with talking Latin Americans studies and political theory (just a recommendation, don't take those classes together in the same semester).

I finished that semester strong and was ready to take a break. Luck would have it my parents knew I needed a break as well, so they decided to take me on cruise to Latin America, the very place I had just been studying. I would be visiting Costa Rica and Panama. This would be my very first time outside the United States, and I was beyond thrilled to be going and putting a visual to the very places that I had been studying all semester long. I would be ready to come back refreshed and ready to start the second semester strong.

Second semester was also the time to start applying for internships. Since I was a double major, I must complete two internships before graduating college. Since I first visited Washington DC two years before, I wanted to go back so that meant applying for internships in the DC area. I applied with Senator Grassley's office, and my congressperson's office as well. I also applied for a longshot dream internship with the National Federation of Republican woman. I was hoping to get offered one of the internships.

A few months went by, and I got a call from Senator Grassley's office for an interview, as well as my congressperson's DC office. I did my interviews, and it was at least a few weeks more before I heard if I was selected. During this time, I received a call from the National Federation of Republican women; they also wanted to interview me. Now it was time to just wait to see if I would hear anything.

While waiting I visited with our local CBS affiliate KMEG about an opportunity to intern with them, I interviewed that week and was offered an internship in the promotions department. I would be working on making adds and would go on commercial shoots. I would also help with promos. I would start in a few weeks. A few days later I would get a call from the senator's office offering me the internship and I accepted. A day after I was called from my congressperson's office and was offered an internship with him, I turned it down as I accepted the offer from the senator's office and would be going to DC. I was ready to go when a few days later I get a call that would completely complicate my plans.

I got a call from The National Federation of Republican Women the dream internship that I was hoping for. I was selected and offered the internship, and it also paid something, which was rare in the internship world. I asked them for a few days to think about it as I was just offered an internship with my senator's office A few days later I visited with my advisors and my old internship boss with Grassley's staff seeking advice. Most importantly, I looked to God for guidance as He never left me a stray before, and because I was reading a daily devotional email. The Bible verse for that day was Matthew 7:7:8 "Ask and it will be given to you; seek and you will find; knock and the door will be opened to you. For everyone who asks receives; the one who seeks finds; and to the one who knocks, the door will be opened." I took that as a sign, and after the conversations I had with family and friends I made the extremely hard decision to turn down the internship with Senator Grassley's office. I accepted the internship with the National Federation of Republican Women. My dream was coming true; I was heading to Washington D.C and I was blessed to have been offered so many great opportunities.

A few weeks later, I would start my summer off interning for KMEG studios. I loved it there. Everyone was extremely kind and offered great advice. I also got a lot of hands-on experience learning how to shoot and produce promos and commercials for the station. My assignment was to film and produce a spot for our local movie theater. I finished my internship just in time to pack and move to DC for the rest of the summer.

I lived on the campus of George Washington University just three blocks from the White House. I could see the Washington Memorial from my apartment kitchen window. It was surreal, and my roommate was from California, also interning with me. We were vastly different but somehow, we just clicked and made it work. We did everything together and we both wanted to make the most out of our DC experience as we could. We visited the Smithsonian's, Mount Vernon, the National Mall, and even went to the 4th of July events. It was an experience I will never forget. I was sitting at the Lincoln Memorial as the fireworks started; it was the icing on the cake for a perfect experience at our nation's capital.

While I was having a lot of fun, I was also there to work. I helped the NFRW plan their bi-annual conference. I also helped research policy issues and helped with data collection. I was given challenging work and loved every second of it. I did miss my family, especially my nephew and niece. I knew though that I had to take this chance for myself, or I would regret it. I am so happy I did. A few weeks into my internship, I received an email that I was awarded the Ronald Reagan Future Leadership Award and Scholarship. I was thrilled and honored, and the award reception would be in DC while I was still there. My parents drove out to pick me up and attended the reception with me. That evening I even got to meet the former President's son. God sure had blessed me and was supplying me amazing experiences.

The experiences that I had while living in DC were more than just living in a new city. I learned more about myself and the person I wanted to become and the goals I wanted to achieve. I learned that although I have had many setbacks and complications living with Turner syndrome, I can still achieve my goals. Five years earlier as a sophomore in high school, I was simply told that this would never happen for me, that college was not an option for me. Fast forward, and five years later I was getting ready to start my senior year of college. Not only was I handling the challenges of one major, I was a double major. I also was going to now be the President of Morningside Civic union and Student Advocate for the Morningside College Student Government, along with the other organizations I belong to.

Senior year was the most challenging and rewarding year yet. I was selected as a member of the senior homecoming royalty. I was honored and shocked; I was always wanting to fit in and be accepted among classmates and friends for so long and to have them not only accept me but think enough of me to select me for homecoming royalty was just an amazing moment. I will always treasure this and be grateful to have these experiences.

I was also now the director for KMSC radio and would be interviewing and covering all the candidates that visited campus who were running for office. I covered stories from local elections to national elections. I got to cover then Senator Obama's campaign stop. I even got to interview Senator John McCain and Chris Dodd. I also interview Governor Mitt Romney's son and many others. This proved that I didn't have to live in DC to have these types of experiences.

I loved preparing for the interviews and asking the tough questions. I was in the press room with members of the national press; I mean, I was literally standing next to a reporter I have watched for years on national media. If that wasn't nerve-racking enough, Senator McCain pointed to me, and it was now time for me to ask him a question. I was completely overcome with nerves but managed to get out my question on how to make college more affordable. He quickly smiled and answered my question and moved on to the next reporter. I couldn't believe in a room of national press the senator took the time address me. It was a moment that I knew I loved journalism. It was also the moment though that I knew I loved campaign work even more.

As I was preparing for the interviews, I would look and around and see all the campaign staff busy, as if they were always in crisis mode and always one step ahead of the next meeting or campaign stop. I thought it was just fascinating to watch and knew I wanted to be a part of that and looked at opportunities to be more involved in the day-to-day operations of campaigns.

As senior year started to end, I was preparing for college graduation and looking into the future. I applied and was accepted to the University of Northern Iowa Public Policy Program and was considering attending, but I kept thinking of how much I loved the campaign work I was doing and knew at least this time it was something that I would be more interested in. After much prayer and reflection, I decided to apply for political campaigns. A few weeks before college graduation, I was offered a job overseeing campaign walkers for the Iowa Republican Party. I would start shortly after college graduation.

Now all I had to do was focus on finishing strong and prepare to hand over the leadership to the organizations I was running. As I started to send out the invitations to my graduation ceremony, it suddenly hit me that I did what was unthinkable to some. I received a college degree, and I did so with a 3.1 GPA. It was a full circle moment many years in the making. All the struggles and long study hours I put into this were worth it. All the times I came home in tears in high school because I was told this was never going to happen for me were now turning into tears of joy as my goals and dreams were coming true.

A few weeks later, I walked across the stage, got my diploma, and looked up to my parents and saw them both beaming with pride, just as they always had at any of my accomplishments. However, this felt different. This was one that proved to be at times the most difficult. It also proved to be the most rewarding. The four years I spent at Morningside College changed my life for the better. As I often say, God doesn't look to better your past, He looks to better your future. I knew that He was guiding me through all those trials and tribulations to help see me through them, making me stronger than I ever thought I could be.

I started college unsure of what I would experience. Now I was leaving Morningside ready to face the world and had a newfound confidence that I could go out there and carry out the goals I had set for myself. Mostly importantly, though, it gave me a passion for lifelong learning and a dedication to help the community I lived in become a better place.

CHAPTER 6

Stepping Out of My Comfort Zone

The few weeks after college I was busy preparing for my new job working through the course of the 2008 campaign for the Iowa GOP, and I would be helping with voter contacts. This was not new for me; I had been volunteering for national and local political campaigns since I was sixteen, so this wasn't new. The only thing new was that I was now a paid employee and was overseeing a group of walkers. If you are not aware of what a campaign office is like, think of an episode of *The West Wing*. It might not be as dramatic, but it certainly is busy, and you must run on endless amounts of energy.

I was working twelve-hour days and rarely had time to relax. It was a fun, fast paced and full of interesting people coming in and out of the office. It was exactly what I had hoped it would be and I learned a lot over those six months I worked for them. I was involved in setting up and organizing campaign events, also overseeing the voter contact walk program. It was a challenge, and it was also the place of growth. At the end of the six months, I learned so much about myself and what I really wanted. I learned that

I had a passion for politics and the fast-paced environment that came with it.

The most rewarding, exciting, and the most interesting part of it was getting to know and meet national, state, and local leaders.

I even count some of these leaders as close friends. I loved and still love talking policy matters with them. People often say that politics can be divisive, but in Iowa, although policy disagreements can be divisive, will still put the *nice* in Iowa nice. I have dear friends on both side of the aisle, and yes, we have our disagreements, but we are always kind to each other, cheer each other on, and want each of us to be successful. Something I wish we would see more in Washington these days.

While working for those leaders, I served as county chair for the Governor's reelection campaigns, county chair for three Presidential campaigns, and I helped with friends who were running for office themselves at almost every level of government. With each campaign, I gained more knowledge and genuinely loved each campaign that I worked on. I became friends with some amazing leaders and truly cherished those conversations that I had. Those few years after college, I gain a wealth of knowledge from those leaders and with each conversation on policy matters, I realized policy was my true passion but how to best use that passion would take time. I knew for certain I wanted to be more involved I just wasn't sure exactly what I wanted to do yet. As with anyone who is fresh out of college, you tend to go on a journey of truly finding your calling, and I was no exception to this.

I knew I was passionate about my community and kids

with special needs, and I was prolife. I also wanted to raise awareness for Turner syndrome, I just needed to find the best way to use my passion to make an impact. That came in the summer of 2011 when I started the path to becoming an advocate for Turner syndrome awareness. In late winter of 2010, I began research on how to spread awareness of Turner syndrome. As I researched, I realized that so much was unknown on Turner syndrome and that there was a campaign to work to spread awareness in several states.

The campaign was that this state would declare February as Turner Syndrome Awareness Month. As I did research, I noticed Iowa was not a state that had yet to declare so I worked with my state representative on the process. For a few weeks, I would work with him on drafting a proclamation. I looked up what other states did and tried to make it my own as well. I was even interviewed by a local news station on bringing awareness to Turner syndrome. A few weeks after sending the draft to my state house representative, I was asked to appear on the floor of the Iowa House. I had been to the state capital many times since the age of five and each time I was always in owe of its beauty and the important work that was carried out in this building.

This time, though, it was different. The very people that I was in awe of growing up were now my friends, and I had even helped many of them on the campaign trail since I started in politics at the age of sixteen. Now I was going to be on the house floor as something I had worked extremely hard on was becoming a reality. My proclamation was going to be read and hopefully pass. I was thrilled that not only did it pass, it was voted unanimously by the Iowa House. It was an emotional moment for me; my parents were with me to hear it read and voted on. My friends who I have been in politics with for many years were the sponsors of the proclamation. What was the most rewarding was the legislators asking me questions and taking an interest in what I had to say and what Turner syndrome was. I was honored to give a voice for this disorder.

The next step I did was to work with the governor's office to start the process of getting him to sign the proclamation. I sent it to his chief of staff, and a few days later started the process of working with him on the proclamation. For about a week we finished outlining the details, and the governor signed the proclamation. It was an amazing moment for me, and I even have them hanging proudly in my home.

It hangs as a reminder on the bad days of this disorder when I am feeling ill, burnt out, and of course when it is a nothing-is-going-my-way day that I at least accomplished this important goal and brought some needed attention to Turner syndrome.

While I did bring some much-needed attention to Turner syndrome, I also wanted to help and get more involved in my community. The only thing was I wasn't sure where to start. I was interested in planning and zoning, so I thought about applying to be a part of that committee. I was interested in bringing more events and activities to the area, so I thought about applying for the parks and recreation committee. I was even interested in the city budget and finances as well.

With the uncertainty of what I wanted to get more involved in, I started attending the city council meetings. I wanted to get up to date on the projects and hoped that it would lead me to helping in the community. I attended for several months and still was not certain; I was going back and forth on what I wanted to do. One day while I was on a walk I was approached by a family friend who asked me about my interests in politics. I was beginning to share that I had been attending the city council meetings and how I wanted to get more involved. Her response changed my life and put me on a journey I never envisioned for myself.

She simply said, "Nicole, why don't you run for city council?"

I was taken aback. I was only twenty-five and due to Turner syndrome, I looked about six years younger than my age, so the idea of running for office myself never occurred to me. I literally laughed when she brought the suggestion up. I mean who would take someone so young seriously? She said, "Nicole, I am serious, you should do it."

I thanked her for her confidence in me, but I wasn't ready to run for office just yet.

I returned from my walk and relayed the conversation to my parents, and to my surprise, they were not surprised at all that someone would mention it to me to run for office. My parents even thought it was a great idea. My parents said, "Give it some thought; you wanted to get more involved in the community. Now is your chance to do so."

My dad said before making the decision I should visit with my friends in politics. They both said I should pray on it before making such a big decision.

That was a great idea, as the Republican State Convention was just a week away and it would have meant I would have a chance to visit with them. One of the people I admire most was then the Lieutenant Governor, and I always loved our visits so I asked her for advice and her thoughts on whether

I should step in the arena of public office. She said that I of course should, in her words, "Go for it." During the convention, I also visited with several of my friends and neighbors to get their feedback, and all of it was positive and informative.

I left that convention inspired and determined and was strongly considering making a run for city council. I visited with my family and friends over the next few weeks, and after thinking it over for several weeks, I decided to do as my friend said and go for it. In August of 2011, at the age of twenty-five I announced that I was seeking a city council seat for the city of Sergeant Bluff.

This would prove to be one the biggest challenges I would face. Not only was I running, but I was running against two popular incumbents, a popular local businessperson, and a community leader who I had not yet had the chance to meet. As I started my campaign, I often felt doubt about myself and the ability to win and even serve. A lot of it was that I still would often hear my former teacher's words about being successful post high school, and to be honest, it still affected me seven years later. I was successful in college and had achieved a great deal, but still her words would creep up and cause me to doubt myself and what I could achieve.

Then I would visit with an elderly man who was concerned about his property taxes rising and worrying he may not be able to afford to stay in his home, or the new family who is renting unable to afford the rising cause of homes and reliable affordable housing in the area. Because I would visit with concern members of the community, I realized that I could in fact help bring these issues to light. Even if I didn't get elected, I would still be able to address these issues and help find solutions. We had an amazing community, but there was always room to improve the lives of its citizens and that was what I was trying to do. However, the campaign certainly wasn't always easy, and it never is when one runs for office. Getting some citizens to take me seriously proved to be a challenge.

I faced the common issues, ones any young politician would often face. "I would vote for you, but I want someone with more experience and a little older" or "Are you even out of high school?" The worst one I ever experienced was getting the door slammed in my face as he said, "I don't vote for women ever." Yes, that even happened in small town Iowa. I had more encouraging experiences than negative experiences, and it made it all worth it and I made several new friends along the way.

As the election was coming closer, community leaders wanted to have a town hall forum where people in the community would be able to ask questions of the candidates. If I am completely honest, I was a little intimidated preparing for this. I mean I was the youngest candidate by a good twenty-five years, and I was the only woman running for a council seat at the time, so it felt a little like I was walking into the lion's den.

As the moderator asked each of us questions, it became easier, and I felt a lot more comfortable answering the tough questions. Towards the end of the town hall, I was asked why I wanted to serve this community. That was easy: I simply wanted to make a difference in the community that I grew up in and loved. I left that town hall feeling that I was finally taken more seriously and even some business leaders in the community were surprised that I could go toe-to-toe with the candidate; a lot of them were supporting.

I had lived in this community since I was born and had known many of the attendees since I had started crawling. Some of the attendees were my former teachers, bosses, and of course, were still family friends. Getting them to see me as a candidate and as grown woman was one of the hardest challenges I was facing on the campaign trail.

That night though something changed in them, and they started to see me as the candidate and not the little girl in pigtails they saw win those pageants. I was an adult now, and I had something to offer this community. I was someone to be taken seriously and I could handle the demands of the office.

That night I think was the turning point in my campaign. I was approached more not to just say "hi" and ask how the parents where. I was asked policy questions and my thoughts on budget proposals, ordinances, and the tax levy. It was the breakthrough I had been looking for the past several months. I was finally seen as a strong candidate, and even if I didn't win (let's face it, it was a long shot getting elected), I at least was finally taken seriously and that could only bode well for my future or at least that was the hope.

The final weeks before the election were stressful, fun, and extremely busy all at the same time, and I enjoyed visiting with friends and community members. As it got closer, I started to get the yard signs out and making calls to remind my supporters of polling locations and times. I returned every email and tried to respond to every phone call.

As the election got closer, I did feel the pressure and my health was taking a hit. I was always on the go, so I started to feel sick, and when you're in a local race there is no one to fill in. You want to be at your best but sometimes life happens, and when you have Turner syndrome, getting the flu or flu related sickness is quite common. Even with the flu shot, I was still likely to get it.

Sure enough, a few weeks before the election, I came down with the ear infection and flu combined. Trying to do the last-minute campaign push was horrible, and I was certain I had just put a fork in my chances of being elected. About a week later, I was feeling well enough to start back on the campaign trial, even though I still was not 100 percent. I knew I had to give it my best shot, and finish as strong as I could. I knew being chosen was still a long shot, however I felt like over this campaign, I had already won in so many ways. I was running against two incumbents, a businessperson, and a popular community member, and I was holding my own well.

I had overcome so many obstacles during this campaign cycle, from being taken seriously as a candidate, illness, to just even being a woman. The fact that I was still fighting in this challenging race was a win regardless of what may lie ahead. I had step out of my comfort zone and challenged myself in ways I never thought I would.

CHAPTER 7

Calling Councilwoman Cleveland?

Election day had finally arrived. I had worked so hard over the past five months leading to election day that I felt I did everything I could. All that was left were the last-minute phone calls to supporters to get them to the polls, and of course to vote. I had a positive response when I called supporters, and traffic at the polling locations was very study, which meant large voter turnout. So to me, that was a good sign. Usually when there was a lot of traffic, there was more on the minds of voters then just a simple city election. It could be policy matters or just excitement of the number of candidates that were on the ballot that day.

I was hoping that would translate into votes. That afternoon I went into the polling location as I had just gotten a chance to vote. As I entered the voting booth and I looked at the ballot, there it was in bold printing, Nicole Cleveland, under candidates for city council. This was one of those moments that I had never seen coming, something that seem too far out of reach but seeing my name made it real. I was a candidate, and no matter what the results were that night I felt like I had come so far in my life to reach this moment.

For an infant who was told she never would be able to walk on her own without braces, to the high school student who was told to give up on her dreams of college to the candidate who was told to wait until she was older. For me, I had been told "you can't" so many times in my life that I started honestly believing that I shouldn't. I doubted myself a lot when making decisions. That day seeing my name on the ballot was emotional. It was all those no moments in my life coming back to the surface, and it was validation that I was right to not listen to those noes and to put myself out there. I decided to finally say I could. With that I colored in the circle next to my name and turned in my ballot, and all I had left was to wait until polls closed that evening, and I would know the results.

The waiting game was honestly one of the hardest parts of the process. I kept myself busy returning phone calls and just running around just trying to keep my mind off the election. No matter what I did, I still had my mind on the election. I kept looking at the time waiting for the polls to close, which were around 8 p.m. It just seemed like it the clock wasn't ticking fast enough, or at least it wasn't fast enough for me.

Finally, around 8p.m. that evening I was driving around the community picking up yard signs. As a candidate, one has only a certain amount of time to remove them from people's yards. I had a few people pass by me with thumbs up and honking; I was starting to get a good feeling. I was certain that I maybe outperformed what I was thinking. I was hoping that I would have at least enough votes to make a good showing. I was hoping to not be the person who received the least number of votes. All I was shooting for was a realistic yet strong performance that night. I was a realist, and I knew going up against two incumbents, and it was hard to beat one let alone two. It was certainly an uphill battle. Suddenly my cell phone started blowing up with text saying it was looking good and congratulating me on how I was doing. When I got home, I pulled up the county auditor's website.

This gave real time election results, and I was shocked when I look at the website, I just kept refreshing it because it didn't seem real what I was seeing. I had won a seat on the City Council, and not only that, I was the highest vote getter. I had outperformed both incumbents and once again had beaten the odds 1. My parents were with me, and I was thrilled to share this with them.

It is an overwhelming feeling when a community puts its faith in you to serve them and their best interest.

Not only was I elected that evening I was informed that I was the youngest woman to ever hold elected office in my city and county history. I also knew that I was the only woman at the time to be on the council. With that, I knew would come a lot of expectations, more than the other council members who served. I knew that even though I had their support I would never take it for granted and would always look out for the best interest of the community and its citizens. With each decision, I would lean on God for guidance.

The next few days following the election were terribly busy, and I was excited to get started. The day after the elections was full of interviews. I was interviewed by the local NBC affiliate and our local newspaper. I was asked a variety of questions about my goals and what I was looking to change. I was direct and honest. I wasn't looking to come to the council and make sweeping changes. I wanted to simply be more involved and wanted my generation to have a greater voice in the decisions being made. I had no axe to grind. I had lived in this community my whole life, and I wanted to see our community grow and prosper. That was all; I was not out to make any substantial changes.

A lot of people thought I was going to come to the council meetings guns blazing, trying to change everything and suggest radical reforms. Some thought because of my age that I was seeking power. In fact, before I even took the oath of office, I received a letter asking me to resign because I was in over my head. I thought, *how can I even be over my head when I haven't even voted on a single issue?* As I read the letter, it became clear that this was just another example of many of people underestimating me and telling me I couldn't. I just took a deep breath and said to myself, "I can do this, and I will prove I can I have proven them wrong before God please see me through"

Soon it was time to take the oath of office. I stood in front of my fellow council members, citizens, and my family and took the oath of office. Then I was seated as a councilwoman, and it was time to get to work. Our meetings were every two weeks, and I would have a packet delivered to my door the Friday before the meetings. Each packet would have the agenda, updated expenditures, and several proposals. With each packet, I spent the weekend going over it, and on Monday I would call the department heads if I had questions. On Tuesday, I was prepared for our bi-weekly meetings. I was new to this and there was a learning curve, as there would be for anyone first taking office. The first major challenge was the budget planning sessions.

This was a challenge as each department has valid and not unrealistic requests for items and improvements. Unfortunately, we could not approve them all, and tough decisions had to be made. I was certainly learning that I couldn't make everyone happy, and for the people-pleaser in me that was hard to accept.

One example was when I first got on the council, a few members thought that I would vote along with them and basically be a yes person for them and their agenda. When it became clear to them I was not a yes person, it caused a lot of tension. For the first six months on the council, we often butted heads, and I even had pencil thrown at me and they would leave a council meeting before it was completed. I often left thinking, *what did I get myself into?* After six months they suddenly resigned, and with two new members to the council it brought some substantial changes, and I was getting into the swing of things. As a council, we were able to accomplish more now and positive changes were happening. I felt like our community was starting to see real progress, and it was all for the better. We didn't raise the tax levy, and we were still able to expand our quality-of-life programs. It was so rewarding to see real growth and positive change in our community.

As a community we were thriving, and I was as excited to be a part of it. As things were progressing on the community front, personal things were progressing too. I had been on the council for almost a year when I received an email that I had been appointed by the Governor of Iowa to serve as a member for the State Vocational Rehabilitation Council. I was honored to be appointed, and I got to help those with special needs, something that was important to me. It was for a three-year term, and I would meet every three months at the State Capital.

I was welcomed with open arms and each meeting bought so much fulfillment and hope. Our goal was to give each person who was receiving aid a better quality of life, and often we would hear those amazing stories of how vocational rehabilitation had changed their lives, and it just brought to the surface how important the work we were doing was.

Between serving on the board, city council, a full-time job, and a variety of organizations I was involved in, I was extremely busy and personal time with friends often took a back seat. The fulfillment I had serving my state and community was beyond what I ever imagined it could be. I was seeing the projects I had helped support come to completion, and I was proud that I had a small part in seeing these projects come to life. Also, the joy I had seen in those whose lives were touched by the services we provided through the State Rehabilitation Council often was an emotional experience, and I got so much more out of it than I felt I had put into it.

While being on the city council was rewarding, it also had its challenges. I certainly had my share of emails and calls from concerned citizens, and I did my best to always address them. Sometimes I was able to resolve those; other times I was not. Those times I did not, I did my best to make them understand their concerns were valid and that I had to look out for the best interest of our community and its citizens. I explained what lead me to make the decision that I did.

Most of the time they would understand and granted

they wouldn't always be happy, but they understood, and most of the time we ended the conversation on good terms. A lot of these were growing pains as a community. We were a small community that was growing fast, and with that meant making challenging decisions that were at the time considered controversial. With each decision and vote, I was growing stronger and stood firm to my convictions. In many ways I was growing along with the city. I was young, naive, and still had so much to learn. I now was a few years into my first term, and I was feeling more confident in my role and that I was making the right decisions.

This was not to say those decisions didn't weigh heavily on me and at times would keep me up at night. How I would vote would affect the entire community as a whole, and I never took that lightly. A lot of citizens don't understand how much time and energy goes into serving on the council. They see the council debate and vote at our biweekly meetings, but many didn't see the amount of time that went into preparing for meetings and votes. The visits, emails, and meetings with department heads were all what I called the behind-the-scenes moments that no one really saw. In all honesty, I didn't even know before taking office, but I learned. I started to feel like I was coming into my own and felt that I was ready to take on more responsibility.

While I was growing into my role as a council member, I was also challenging myself more personally too. I was starting to take on bigger roles in state and national campaigns. I was endorsing candidates, which was something I never did before. I mean, I had worked for them and had shared my support; however, there was something special about being asked to officially endorse a candidate. It was the feeling I was being taken seriously and that my opinions had value. I was even attending rallies and campaign events as an elected official and even got to introduce some leaders to the area. I was becoming more confident in my own skin.

At times, though, that confidence would be tested, and as I did put myself out there more politically, with that also came more criticism for who I supported and what issues I supported. I certainly had to learn to, as my dad would say, "grow a thick skin." It took a while to learn this, and in all honesty was one of the hardest parts of being in politics. I knew it was part of being in politics, and I was used to it being one of the few women in local government. I was also used to the certain kind of talk that came with being in a male dominated field such as politics. I was not prepared though for the type of cruel and crude comments I would have come my way. They were often personal and not related to my policy decisions. I learned to ignore them most of the time, but it still stung and when it came from people you knew it was harder to process. I would pray that God would open their hearts and minds to Him in ways only He could.

I was growing, and so was our community. We had boomed economically, and we were growing in population too, and with that brought growing pains. More need for affordable housing, new streets, revising city guidelines, and making sure that we had the equipment needed to handle the growth. It was an exciting time in our community and being part of it was an honor, and it was something truly special.

The first four years of holding elected office I learned so much about myself, more than I ever thought I would. I came to elected office naïve in a lot of ways, unsure of myself and my role. I had to learn as I went. I was developing into the type of elected official I wanted to be. I spent many hours reading and preparing for each council meeting, and I was as prepared as I could be, but of course there would always be something that would put a hitch in your preparation, Project delays or increase cost, staff changes, and, of course, natural disasters.

It happened in September of 2014. We had what was called a microburst. It is like a tornado and causes almost as much damage. It certainly did a lot of damage to our community. While some areas were unaffected, some were severely damaged. Over million dollars' worth of damage, if I remember correctly. The area with the most damage was our local cemetery. That night, I went on ride along with our city emergency staff and the damage was something I had never seen before. Some roads were blocked, and some areas were dangerous and needed to be addressed right away. It took almost a month for things to start to look normal. Over a few days, I took off work to volunteer and help in areas of greatest need.

A few days after the storm, my grandmother got extremely ill and suddenly passed away in the middle of the aftermath of this storm, causing a storm in myself. My grandmother lived next door and was my last surviving grandparent, and she was someone I often went to for advice and support. Now I was dealing with the struggle of a major loss in my life and one of the biggest challenges in my tenure as a council woman. I had to put my emotions aside and put our community first, and that was what I did. I of course was there for the family, but my grandmother was someone who always put others first and never thought about herself. Even after my grandfather passed, she stood strong and put on a brave face for her children and grandchildren, so I knew she would want me to do so as well and keep moving forward. It was extremely hard to do but helping with clean up and volunteering made me feel more connected to her and helping was also comforting in many ways. God was supplying me the refuge I needed.

After a few months things started to slow down, and we were able to focus on and go back to working on the projects and plans we had to set aside during this clean up. We had some major projects that were in full swing. I was also entering my final year of my first term, and it was getting close to deciding if I would seek reelection.

I still had a few months to decide, and I was going back and forth on this. I didn't want to, as I would say to others, overstay my welcome. I did want to see those projects through and felt like I had still a lot to offer. As it got closer to deciding, I was asked more often if I would consider running for another term. After much consideration, prayer, and reflection, I decided to put my name on the ballot once again hoping the community would be calling on Councilwoman Cleveland to continue to serve.

CHAPTER 8

Second Time Around and Knowing When To Move On

Running for reelection was an entirely unique experience compared to when I first ran four years earlier. I was now the incumbent, and I had four years of experience. I had tough decisions and votes behind me. I wasn't the naive recent college graduate that was asking people to take a chance on me. I had been tested, I had grown, and I was prepared for the next four years. When I turned in my paperwork, I was told I would be running unopposed. I appreciated the support and faith in me, but I never took it for granted.

I held a reelection kickoff event to thank my early supporters and to give them an update on what my plans for the next four years if I was lucky enough to be reelected to the city council. It was a great turn out, and I was grateful for the support I had received. I was endorsed by my state representative, state senator, and even the lieutenant governor. She even did a video on my behalf. That was truly an honor, and I was grateful to have their support. To have their faith in me and the decisions I had made over my first term meant the world to me, and I would never forget it. Now it was time to start getting to work on the campaign.

I door knocked on almost every house and made phone calls to not just ask for support but to also ask the citizens what we could do as a council to further improve and open the line of communication with them. Visiting with members of our community was one of the biggest joys I had serving as a city council member. So many of them would invite me into their homes to visit. Even on Saturdays when college football was on, they would invite me to watch the game. That was what made our community so special--the kindness among people is something all too rare in big cities and why I chose to stay in my community and wanted to continue to serve it.

The day had arrived, election day, and I was just as nervous as I was when I first run. I was unopposed but it didn't mean that a strong write in campaign could be out there and shake things up. That is how our mayor won his seat was on a write in campaign, so it was not out of the possibility that someone could do the same. Now it was a waiting game again, and I would soon find out if I had the support of the community again or not. My parents and I decided to go to the county auditor's office to watch the results.

A few minutes after the polls closed the county auditor came up to me and said, "Congratulations, Nicole, you have been reelected." I was thrilled, honored, and humbled to be chosen. To have the community's faith entrusted in me not once but twice was a truly special, and I knew to never take their support or concerns for granted.

I started off my second term building on the promises we made as a council, and economic development was at the forefront of our priorities this term. As a community, we have seen a large amount of population growth in our area and now it was time to focus on amenities and expanding business opportunities in our community to supply goods and services for our growing community. It was a busy time in our community and with that brought new challenges and ways to learn and grow.

I also built on the relationships that I had with other local leaders, and this was always a wonderful way to seek out advice, ideas, and recommendations for future projects and events. I was honored to be chosen to represent my community on our annual Chamber of Commerce trip to Washington DC. For three days I meant with our senators and their staff. Held meetings with congressional aids and federal agencies. It was very productive, and we did receive results from those meeting. I was thrilled to be able to bring those resources back to our community.

One of those projects that were discussed was the major revamping of the old air force housing that had been turned into a large rental property several decades earlier and needed major repairs. Of course, those repairs were expensive, and we worked with the property owners to develop a plan to repair each rental property within a certain amount of time knowing that it would be at least seven years to complete this project.

This was a project was close to my heart. I grew up living in this very area. I played in the very park that had not been updated since before I was even born. As a family, we had moved to a different area of our community several years earlier, so before visiting with residents of this area, I was unaware of how bad the conditions had gotten since I had moved. I knew I wanted to do something about it and so did the council; we worked out a development agreement with new ownership. They are currently working on improving those conditions one unit at a time.

We even organized a cleanup day with the members of that area. We cleaned up the ditches and even cut down shrubs and trees that were causing issues in the park. It was a great feeling to be more hands on. It was nice to work with fellow concern citizens and to give back more of my time and energy and seeing the proof that we were making a difference. Going through my health issues, I often wondered why God had me endure some of those struggles. My parents would always trust in Him knowing He has a plan. I prayed often for Him to show me His plan and to give me hope when I was in those darkest days of my disorder.

Days like the park cleanup were one of those days I truly felt that He was guiding me and showing me that making a difference in people's lives was part of His plan. At times in my life, I had struggled with this. If He had a plan, why didn't He just show me instead of making me go through so much? Then somedays He would show me that I was on the right track, I just needed to learn to listen.

I would take that spirit as I continued serving the community, and each day was different and brought with it more challenges and opportunities than the first term did. I enjoyed each moment of it and was happy I never stuck to my original plan of being a professional ballet dancer at age six. It would have been fun, but for me, not as fulfilling.

Life certainly was unexpected, and one of those moments was being nominated for the prestigious Siouxland 10 Under 40. This is an honor given to those in our region under forty who are making a strong positive impact on our community. I was thrilled to be nominated, but I knew it was very selective and the possibility of being chosen as one of the ten was slim, so I was just enjoying being nominated. I was grateful the local business owner thought enough of me to nominate me.

Several weeks after being informed that I was nominated, I received an email stating that I had been chosen as one of Siouxland's 10 under 40. I was thrilled and honestly shocked. I knew so many great people more deserving than me; in fact, I even nominated someone who I felt deserved it more. I rushed and called my parents as I was too excited to wait until I was off work to tell them. I would have to wait to tell others until it was published in the local magazine that I was honored as one of the 10 under 40.

A few days before publication of the issue, the magazine hosted a reception in our honor, and we were able to invite guest to attend. I, of course, invited my parents, and they were there for me when I received this honor. This was also the night that I would get to meet the other nominees. Some of the honorees I had known for a long-time, while others I had the pleasure of meeting for the first time. When each honoree was called, they would highlight their accomplishments, and I was in awe of each of them and the amazing work they were doing. I could not believe I was a part of it.

Then my name was called, and I was honored. It was surreal for me. For this small-town girl who had been through so many obstacles growing up, days like this were something I never thought this would happen to me. I never thought that I would serve my community, let alone be honored for doing so. This was special and a highlight of my time serving on the city council. I have it displayed proudly in my home to remind me on those bad days to never give up on your dreams.

When the publication came out, I had family and friends call, text, and email me with congratulations and to share in the joy with me. I just could not believe the amount of support I was getting. It was overwhelming and made me feel truly blessed. It made me feel valued, appreciated, and that I could really achieve my dreams. I just had to have faith in myself and, as it says in Philippians 4:13, "I can do all things through Christ who strengthens me." I just had to lean on Him to guide me.

One of those times came when I was asked by members of city staff and the community if I would consider making a run for mayor of our community. I had a good relationship with our fellow council members and even the mayor. When I was asked by a few members of the community, I simply told them the truth. I wasn't looking to make the run for higher office, I was happy being able to serve my community as their council member. I would address their concerns and thank them for their support and the conversation would often end there. I knew some members of the community were not thrilled with some of the decisions that were being made and that was nothing unusual; you will never make everyone in the community happy.

One day as election was getting closer, one member of the city staff contacted me and began laying out concerns about our mayor and asked me if I consider a run to challenge him. I went home that day with a heavy heart not sure what I should do. I had a great relationship with him and did not want to tarnish that. I wrestled with the decision, and I prayed on it for several days just hoping He would give some guidance as to what I should do.

I took out the paperwork uncertain if I was going to turn it in. I knew if I went ahead with running, I would likely be opening myself to up to a lot of attacks and would face the hardest campaign I would ever have to face. A few days before the election I received a threating phone call from the mayor trying to convince me not to run and telling me that he would ruin my political future. It was that moment that I knew I had to run because the type of concerns that were raised and the way I was being treated proved that I had to at least challenge him.

I turned in my paperwork, and it was official I was a candidate for mayor. Normally this would be an exciting moment as I was trying to challenge myself and seek higher office. This was not one of those moments for me. I was challenging someone who I had known and respected my whole life, and seeking this office weighed heavily on my shoulders. I now was committed and would give one hundred percent of myself to it.

I approached this campaign the way I did with all the others. I focused not on the negative but simply what I could bring to the table and what I would like to see accomplished if I was elected as mayor. It was a hard campaign, and I would often get threatening emails, text, and phone calls. I was also subjected to negative attacks and smear campaigns. I would get calls from supporters asking why I was for this or against that because they were told I was. It was hard to stay focus and calm while so much misinformation was being spread about me. I took the high road and would handle it with the grace and professionalism that one should have while for office. I asked God to give me strength to get me through it, and He did.

Not to say that it was easy. It was extremely difficult hearing those remarks being made and knowing that people who you thought were friends being the ones making them. I was even told I had done nothing for this community. This was heartbreaking. I got involved serving my community because I loved it. I felt that I was being called to do so. It was the place where I grew up; it was and will always be my home, and I cared about the citizens of this community. To hear I have done nothing for it was devasting, and it was meant to be cruel. Some didn't like that I challenged the status quo That I had the audacity to stand up for myself and other members of the community.

I knew when I ran it was going to be the hardest campaign I would ever have to fight and knew that I needed to lean on my faith to get me through those tough times. I knew there was a reason God was having me go through this. I just needed to have faith that whatever happened in this election, it would be up to Him and the people of my community.

When election day came, I was at peace. I ran a positive campaign and did everything thing I could. It was up to the voters. That night I lost my first election, and as the results came in, I wasn't upset or ashamed. Had I wish the results would have been different? Absolutely anyone who runs wishes they would win, but I consider myself a winner for standing up and being brave enough to not back down and to withstand the smear and threats that were coming my way.

This election taught me that I was stronger than I thought, and that even though I lost, it was worth taking a risk. I was always cautious when taking big leaps and making big decisions, mainly being that when I was told so often that I couldn't do something, it stuck with me. This experience taught me that although taking a risk might not always bring the outcome I wanted, but it could teach me more about myself. I think that was what God was trying to show me. I was at peace with this. As it is written in John 14:27, "Peace I leave with you, my peace I will give to you. Not as the world gives do I give to you. Let not your hearts be troubled neither let them be afraid."

The next two years on the council, I served alongside my fellow councilmembers and the mayor, and we put the harsh campaign behind us and continued to work to improve the lives of our community. When it was time to decide if I was going to seek another term on the council, I had some soul searching to do. If I was going to run, it would mean four more years, and it was a major time commitment if I were dedicated to it. I had given so much to the community that I started to lose myself. I was no longer prioritizing my family and friends, and I also had a full-time job outside of being on the council that needed my attention and full focus. It was not an easy decision to give up something that had been a part of my life for over eight years, but I knew it was time to move on and it was time to take a break and recharge.

CHAPTER 9

Learning To Lean on God

Deciding not to seek reelection to the city council and take a brief step back from politics in 2019 was one of the hardest decisions I had to make, and it took a lot of soul searching. It was a part of who I was since I was sixteen years old and was something I truly had a passion for. I loved my community. I wasn't leaving on bad terms. I wasn't leaving because I had just came out of a rough campaign season and lost a hard-fought race. I moved on from that, and I had worked and ran many campaigns and knew going in that you can't win them all. I decided not to seek reelection to a third term in large part that in my opinion, a change in leadership regularly is vital for a community to progress. It is because with change brings fresh prospective and ideas. After eight years of serving my community, it was time to move on and let someone else bring their ideas to the table. It simply was time to move on and give myself some time to relax and take a break. In January of 2019, I attended my final meeting as a council member.

The few weeks following my last meeting I honestly just enjoyed the added free time. I had been on the go so much since I was child, and I enjoyed the much-needed free time. I caught up on reading the books on my bookshelf I hadn't gotten a chance to get to (You know, the ones you buy on impulse at Barnes and Noble's). Instead of my weekends reading committee reports and financial disclosures, I was spending time in the kitchen cooking and baking and setting my DVR to *The Pioneer Woman*. I was also catching up with friends as well. I even got a golden retriever puppy. I named him Winston after my favorite political leader Winston Churchill. We traveled out of state to get him, and boy was he worth it. He is such an incredibly special part of our family, and we all love him and spoil him. Soon though, I was getting restless. I was always involved in several organizations and programs that I never sat still; suddenly, I was given this free time and I preferred being busy. I was still busy, but not like I was while on the council. I don't like to sit still, something that I got instilled in me by my parents. I started wanting something more meaningful to fill my time. I was still involved in several organizations and was appointed to a second term on the State Rehabilitation Council, and I did have plenty of meaningful work. The State Rehabilitation Council was just such a rewarding experience and seeing the positive impact we were having on the lives of those with disabilities brought so much joy to me. I left each meeting feeling like the programs and changes we were recommending were truly making a difference in each of their as lives. It was worth the almost three hour trip each way to the state capital to attend each meeting. I knew what I was doing was fulfilling in so many ways, but I couldn't help but feel that something was still missing, and that God was calling me to something more impactful.

Then one day I was on social media browsing posts on a support group for those with Turner syndrome, and as I was reading the stories of how so many of them were not diagnosed until their teen years and how much they had struggled as a result, I realized this was the meaningful work I was looking for. I wanted to shed a light on Turner syndrome. I was a lucky one who had access to prompt treatment, and I wanted to help if I could raise awareness. Now, I just needed to find how I would do that. In 2020, while the world literally was at a standstill, I began to think of creative ways that allowed me to spread awareness but be able to stay home and safe. In the spring of 2020, I began the process of starting a blog that would spread awareness and hope for those who like me who were living with this

While I was starting this, though, my personal life took a drastic and life alerting turn in mid-2020. One day while my father was working, he had severe back pain, and it was so bad he decided to go to the doctor. He just could not take the pain any longer. The doctor said it was likely a kidney stone. That was not uncommon for my father; he had them in the past. They sent him home and told him follow up with a specialist the following day. Overnight it had gotten much worse, and he had begun to fill up with excessive amount of fluid. He was rushed to hospital and after hours of waiting for some answer it was later determined he went into multi organ failure.

This was at the height of COVID-19, and with that it brought visiting restrictions. No one was allowed to visit him, not even my mom. This was so hard on all of us, but especially for me. He was critical, and I was a daddy's girl. My parents were my world and having one of them face a major medical struggle was the hardest thing I have ever had to go through. My father was in the hospital for several days without any of us being able to visit him in person. We all called multiple times a day, and each time I would get off the phone it was so hard. All I wanted to be was by his side, letting him know how much I loved him.

We still are not fully sure what had led to this and likely may not know for certain. When this happened, it put things in to prospective, and I was grateful for the close relationship I had with my father. It also made me realize just how scared my parents must have been after my birth and helpless, as that was how I had felt when I was unable to be by my dad's side. All I could do was pray for him and give our family strength. After eight days in the hospital, my dad was released. Now it was a long road to recovery for him, but he was fighter.

He did well for a few weeks, then one day his heart rate went extremely high, and he was in what the doctor's call atrial fibrillation. This meant that he was in the hospital again for a few days. This time, though, my mom was able to visit him as one person was allowed to visit per day, so this helped lift my dad's spirits and ease my mom's worry as well. They adjusted my dad's medication, and he was finally sent home and has not had any health scares since thankfully.

In fact, he is now feeling better physically than he has in years and just celebrated his seventy-first birthday and is fully retired. I am thankful that my prayers were answered.

Life was getting back to a more normal pace as he was improving, so I started working on the blog more and sharing my journey with others. It was extremely rewarding, and I often got some great questions and ideas by others in the support groups on social media. I enjoyed it and enjoyed getting to know others who were experiencing living with Turner syndrome like I was. Honestly, for the first time I truly felt like someone understood me and what I was going through. I was getting so much more back from writing this blog than I felt like I was giving. I also had more time to devote to it as I was working from home.

In the era of COVID, it also changed the political landscape, making it harder to be as involved as I was before it. This meant that I wasn't as active as I was, and I missed it a lot.

I know, who misses the crazy life that politics brings, especially in today's world?

However, it was a part of who I was for so long that not being a part of it anymore was like a part of who I was, was missing. I slowly started getting back into politics. That did not mean running for office again, it just met that I was going back to my roots, volunteering for those seeking office. I was thrilled to have some routine of normalcy as COVID forced so many changes on us all, and with living with Turner syndrome, my immune system was weakened anyway, so I had to be incredibly careful and stayed home. I was working from home, and I even stay home and zoomed all my meetings during this time. Also, like many of you, that meant watching live streams of church services.

Living with Turner's, one is used to adjusting to changes, as you often have to with this disorder. Adjusting to the changes with COVID were easier than I often thought it would be. I am a people person, so not seeing my friends and extended family face-to-face was difficult, as I am sure it was for anyone. I did treasure my time with my parents, as I was in lockdown with them. I even got to try some new cooking recipes with them too. The vaccine was finally rolling out, and maybe we could get back to normal.

I was excited to be able to somewhat go back to normal

to have a chance to go out with friends and catch up instead of only on Zoom. I was even soon going to being working a few days a week at the office; it was looking like life was back on track for the most part. It felt like to worst of the past year was finally behind us ,and we could move on and get back to our routine.

Then in April of 2021, life took a horrible and life altering turn for our entire family. My mom was experiencing shortness of breath and trouble even walking short distances. She was referred to a cardiologist who suggested she have a catheterization. I was worried, as I knew it was highly likely she would have an obstruction, but I never expected the news I would get when my father called me after the test. My mom needed to have a triple bypass surgery, and it was serious. She would have to stay in the hospital until the surgery, which was in a few days.

On Monday, April 26th, 2021, my mom underwent triple bypass surgery. I was unable to be there due to COVID regulations. Only my father could be there, and it was so hard on our whole family just waiting for any news. After five hours, my dad called me to tell me surgery went well, and she was doing great. We thought that was going to be the worst of our worries and that she would soon be home with us to start her recovery.

A week later, she was still in the ICU with shortness of breath and was losing a large amount of blood. The doctors were not sure where the bleeding was coming from. They soon took her down for emergency surgery. They discovered that one of the new heart grafts had a hole the size of a pin needle, and it was repaired. Now that was taken care of, I began to have hope that this was the only set back and soon my mom would finally be on the road to recovery.

I was heartbroken when a week later my mom was becoming very weak and just wasn't getting better and again losing blood. They rushed her down yet again for surgery, and this time they removed her sternum and discovered a large amount of infection. Further testing would confirm it was MRSA, which is extremely difficult to battle, and my mom was critical but stable as they called it.

Each day that my mom was hospitalized, my father was by her side never leaving her except to go home to sleep at night. Whenever we could and were allowed, my brother and I would go up to see her as well as my sister-in-law, my niece, and nephew. Seeing my mom on a ventilator and largely unresponsive was an image I would never forget. This was the hardest thing our entire family and I have ever had to go through, and my mom was so young and full of life. I wasn't prepared to see her in this condition.

I would go home, and I would cry and pray nonstop just hoping that my mom would improve. Somedays she would improve, and we would have hope, and then other days she would take a turn for the worst, and it was emotionally draining. I just wanted to be able to hug and talk to my mom, and each day I visited, it was harder and harder to leave her knowing she wasn't improving and that it could be the last time I would be able to see my mom.

That worst fear was realized on the morning of June 7th, 2021. Around 1:00 a.m., my father was awakened to a call from the ICU nurse that my mom was bleeding yet again and was already rushed in for emergency surgery. My father woke me up and my brother, and as a family we rushed to the hospital. Around a half hour later, the sergeant came out and explained that my mom's new graft had ruptured as the infection had spread to her heart. He said that they did everything they could, but my mom was dying, and the doctor said that we would be lucky if we had an hour left with her.

We all stood around her in her room holding her hand. I said how much I loved her, and shortly after 3:00 a.m. on the morning of June 7th, 2021, my mom took her final breath on this earth surrounding by our family. She had fought the best she could for forty-five days (about one and a half months) and never once did my father leave her side. He was a pillar of strength for us all. She was only sixty-four years old, and they were married for almost forty-one years. She was the center of our family, and now we would have to face the harsh reality of life without her.

I was beyond heartbroken. My mom was my best friend, and we had an unbreakable bond. I often compared our relationship to that of the *Gilmore Girls*. I could tell her anything and everything and knew she would be by my side. A few months before she passed away, she told me that no matter what happened, she had no regrets with our relationship and that she loved me. That was what was getting through those extremely hard days that I have had ever since she passed away. That and knowing that she was in heaven and that she had such a strong faith made those unbearable days just a little more bearable.

Those hard days are frequent. My mom was my rock, my go-to person, and my confident. I went to her for literally even the smallest things. We had so many traditions together, like every Christmas we would bake together and send baked goods to relatives and friends. Now I must move forward in my life without my mom and try to carry on those traditions for her in her memory. It is hard, but my church and my family have seen my salvation as I transition to a new normal. As a family, our faith has gotten us through those challenging times in the past, and it is what is getting me through it now. As the Bible says, "the lord is near to the brokenhearted," and I feel that he is with me even on the hardest days (Psalm 34:18).

I wished my mom would have been by my side and able to read this book because she was such a vital part of it and wanted me to share my story with others. I knew that as I wrote this book that although she was not physically with me, I could still hear her voice encouraging me to have the strength to do so. Losing my mom was the hardest experience I have ever had to endure.

I know that losing a parent is hard for anyone. So much you wished you could have said or done if only you had more time. Time with loved ones is precious, and you need to treasure the memories and times you have with them, as you never know when life can suddenly take a turn.

That is why I am thankful I had the relationship I had with my mom. I knew she loved me and that I loved her and that I can be at peace knowing this. Same of my father; we have a great relationship, and I am the quintessential daddy's girl. If you are reading this today and have a strained relationship with your parents, it is not too late open your heart to God and to ask forgiveness. You only have one mom and dad, and life is just too short to hold grudges and hate in your heart.

I was blessed that even though I lost my amazing mom, I have nothing but great memories and love when I think of her. She instilled a strong faith in me that has gotten me through those most heartbreaking and challenging times in my life. When my parents were told I may never walk normally, they leaned on God; when we were told of my learning disability, we leaned on God; when I was told that college was not an option, I leaned on God to give me strength and to guide me in what I should do. God may not always give you the answer you are looking for, but He is giving the answer you need and is always guiding you to a more meaningful life.

CHAPTER 10

Being Perfectly Imperfect

It is my sincere hope that what you take away from this book is a feeling of being inspired and the power to believe in yourself.

When it was first suggested by family and friends that I take the time and write a book, I was taken aback. Why would anyone want to read my story? I was not a celebrity, nor had I done anything yet in my life that people would find remotely interesting enough to read. I hadn't climbed Mount Everest, I wasn't an actor or an influencer with thousands of followers on Instagram or Tik Tok. I was just a small-town Iowa girl, and yes, I had some unique experiences, and I cherished those opportunities, but they were certainly not interesting enough to author a book. Then I started thinking about how my story is so much more than mine; it could be anyone's story. Really anyone could relate in some way to what I had to overcome.

Whether it was a medical condition, a learning disability, a loss of a parent, or even dealing with the heartbreak of infertility, I know that so many of you reading this can relate in some way to what I have experienced in my life and think maybe my family was right after all. Maybe I should take a leap of faith and start on this journey of authoring this book.

I knew it was not going to be easy. It never is when putting yourself out there and sharing your story for the entire world to see, and that is certainly true for me.

I frankly was scared to do so; I was sharing some details of my life that very few people were aware of. It was like that presentation in high school again. This though was on a larger scale, and I was sharing parts of my life that I kept private. Some of it I didn't even share with my close friends. I knew it was going to be an adjustment for me, and it truly was. I often thought about abandoning this project several times. It was certainly not easy reliving some of what I had to endure. I knew though that by sharing my story, I would hopefully help shine a light on rare genetic disorders.

I know that so many people are fighting a rare disorder just like I am, and I know how often at times you feel alone, misunderstood, and like no one knows exactly what you are going through on a day-to-day basis. It often feels lonely. Not that you are alone, it's just that the rarity of the disorder makes it often hard to find anyone who is living with it as well, so it is difficult to share what you are experiencing.

That is why I authored this book. I wanted to share my story in hopes that you see yourself and feel encouraged and maybe even feel a little inspired to try something new and out of you comfort zone. I hope you read and say, "If she can do it, why can't I?" So many times, when I was told no, I wish I had someone I could have related to encouraging me and showing me that it was possible.

Yes, my family and friends always encouraged me and often pushed me to reach more of my full potential. They pushed me when I often didn't believe in myself. I had a great support force, but I literally never met anyone else who had Turner syndrome. I didn't see anyone who had the same classic Turner features as I did, and no one that I could look at and see like myself. My friends and family did the best they could to understand but they simply couldn't because they didn't have Tuner syndrome. They were always amazing, but I always wished I could talk to someone who had the same disorder.

There was and frankly still is rarely any media attention to the disorder, and when it is it is often misrepresented. For example, a few years ago a local news affiliate did a report about a young girl with Turner syndrome who was having major heart complications, and I think she needed surgery. The headline said, "Potential deadly syndrome only affects females." While I thank them for bringing much needed awareness and attention to this disorder, this did more harm than good.

For one, although Turner syndrome can cause many complications, it is certainly not terminal, and the headline made it seem like it was. When it is represented, it usually is not represented correctly. Second, when it is represented, it is often mentioned in passing a sound bite on the news and often with mostly generalizations about the disorder spitting out medical jargon that even the most devoted *Greys Anatomy* fans couldn't understand or follow. It always comes from a perfect, put-together reporter who likely never heard of the disorder, so it never really seems like they focus on what truly living with Turner syndrome can be like. That is the main reason I authored this book.

Since not seeking reelection to the city council in 2019, I wanted to change my focus and raise awareness to Turner syndrome. It has been an important mission in my life.

I wanted to raise awareness for research so that earlier diagnosis can bring access to much needed treatment and a higher quality of life. I would like to one day have a conversation about this disorder without the first question being "what is Turner syndrome?" It took me a while to see where I could be the most helpful and bring the most encouragement to those like me who lived with this disorder. Then in the fall of 2020, I took a leap of faith, decided to start a blog, and named it the Butterfly Chronicles (hints the name for this book). Now you most likely have been wondering through *The Butterfly Chronicles*, "What do butterflies have to do with Turner syndrome?" In the Turner syndrome community, Turner syndrome patients are often referred to as butterflies. We are because, like the butterfly, we are considered rare, fragile, and beautiful one-of-a-kind miracles. I wanted to bring that same spirit when I started the blog.

I had a lot of positive feedback from those in the Turner syndrome community. So much so that I decided to share my journey in more depth in hopes that it would give a true real-life reflection of what living with this disorder was like with honesty and with real experiences. None of the medical jargon often in many of the books published on the topic of Turner syndrome. This can often overwhelm parents who are just starting out on this journey of having a daughter diagnosed.

This book was certainly not going to be that. I wanted it to be a personal experience; just myself sharing my story with you and simply wanting to bring comfort to those families who are starting out on this journey of having a daughter who is newly diagnosed or to the young woman who just was diagnosed. Living with Turner syndrome is not easy, and yes it can be scary, but it is not a life sentence and one can achieve a great deal despite the challenges this disorder brings. In fact, I have come to celebrate that I am a Turner syndrome warrior, and in time you will too. I truly hope you do.

I celebrate the person I am: all the good, the bad, and the ugly parts because I survived the odds and I know that I am here for a reason. All the experiences I have had led me to be able to be brave enough to open and share my story. The amazing experiences I have had, the heartache, and the struggles have made me the woman I am today, and without those experiences, I may not have been able to open and share this crazy wonderful journey with you all. I used to be very private about living with this disorder, afraid of what people would think if they knew I had it. I have said, and I mean it, throughout the book that I wasn't ashamed of living with Turners, I just knew it would open a conversation I wasn't ready to have. I did not want them to look at me and possibly see me as fragile because I knew I was anything but.

If you take away anything from my story, it is to not be afraid to share your health journey because when you do you will realize that you will have so much support and love from those who genuinely care about your wellbeing and success. You will learn that these people will be there for you in the good times and in life's struggles. I hope you also realize to advocate for yourself, don't let others decide your journey for you. Paint your own masterpiece, and you will be surprised just how colorful and vibrant the world can really be. You just have to be your perfectly imperfect self and open yourself to the possibilities. I want you to genuinely believe that with God all things are possible.

Endnotes

1 Full House, season 4, episode 16, "Stephanie Gets Framed," directed by Joel Zwick, aired Jan. 25, 1991, on ABC, https://www.hbomax.com/series/urn:hbo:series:GYS_I_wTdDa6NwwEAAAAC.